Let Love Go
FORWARD

from this time and place

*Encouragement for
Your Marriage*

TERRY OLSEN

REDEMPTION
P R E S S

Published by Redemption Press, PO Box 427, Enumclaw, WA 98022
Toll-Free (844) 2REDEEM (273-3336)

Redemption Press is honored to present this title in partnership with the author. The views expressed or implied in this work are those of the author. Redemption Press provides our imprint seal representing design excellence, creative content, and high-quality production.

The references and addresses in this book are accurate at the time of publication. They are provided as resources. Some material in various chapters in this book has been selected from material that appeared in my first book, *My Father, My Hero: Becoming Your Child's Best Friend.* 1994, WinePress Publishing, Enumclaw, Washington.

ISBN 13: 978-1-68314-770-1
ePub ISBN: 978-1-68314-771-8
Kindle ISBN: 978-1-68314-772-5

Library of Congress Catalog Card Number: 2018955755

Let Love Go FORWARD

from this time and place

*Encouragement for
Your Marriage*

This book is dedicated to

Mardi,

wonderful wife and faithful companion

with caring compassion and intuitive wisdom.

I am blessed beyond measure.

Endorsements

"Terry and I have been friends for over fifty years. He lives out these scriptural maxims. He tells his story with humility and grace, and calls all of us to follow Jesus's commands to love, forgive, encourage, and serve. We would be wise to heed his gracious and encouraging words about love, marriage, and relationships."

—Doug Burleigh, former president of Young Life
currently with The Fellowship in Washington, DC

"I have known Terry for many years; he is truly an example to follow. He has been a great influence to many men, including myself. In this simple book, he gives guidance and hope from his experiences and a life well lived. I highly recommend this book."

—Gregory L. Jantz, PhD, founder of The Center— A Place of Hope
author of thirty-five books

"Newlyweds and oldie-weds alike: Terry Olsen's tips on dipping out and refilling your 'love bucket' are timeless. He proves that the simplest things are often the most important."

—Dori and Suzanne Monson
friends and encouragers to many

Table of Contents

Acknowledgments

Many friends have contributed to my knowledge and understanding of the marriage journey. There are too many to name, but I have so much appreciation for all those who have befriended me over many years through the good times and the difficult times. We have all had our share, and when people are transparent in their fears and struggles, friendships deepen. I genuinely appreciate all their contributions to my life. Specifically, a big thank-you to my wife, Mardi, for her proofreading and her wise and appreciated insights. Also, many thank-yous to the following for their willingness to preview the manuscript: Jack and Jill Miller, Doug and Debbie Burleigh, Dick and Arlene Warne, Dori and Suzanne Monson, Gregory Jantz, Lizbeth Rogers, Craig Hertz, Caitlin Philbrick, Amber Getta, and Josh Bishop. Their insights and suggestions have been invaluable.

I also want to specifically thank all those who have helped in the publishing of this book. The entire Redemption Press team has been so helpful from start to finish and has provided a quality publication. I have grateful praise for all those at Redemption Press.

When searching for a title to best express what I wanted to convey in this book, I remembered hearing a song by my friend Mark Pearson, "Let Love Go Forward." It fit perfectly. This is exactly what I had hoped this book would encourage. Mark Pearson is an accomplished singer, songwriter, recording artist, and all-around one of the nicest people you will ever meet. Mark is not only an accomplished professional, but he is also warmly personal. You feel his music in his concert performances.

Mark also sings and plays guitar and banjo with The Brothers Four, a longtime folk-singing group entertaining audiences worldwide and still going strong after sixty years. A special thank-you to Mark for all his good music over the years and for his words that capture the heart and the essence of this book. Mark can be contacted at MarkPearsonMusic.com.

Introduction

Hope is a powerful ally. When it comes to the marriage relationship, we live in a world of hope from the day we first became interested in that special person, especially as that bonding and exciting chemistry bubbles to the surface. Our most extravagant hope or dream is to see this bonding move on through our wedding and for the rest of our journey here on earth. Unfortunately, as much as hope is our ally and expectation, reality often deals a different hand.

This is the story of two people who choose to bond together in friendship—a friendship they are trusting to last a lifetime. How can you describe that feeling of constant joy, of being loved, of being cared for, of feeling safe in the arms of another's warm embrace, of having your love bucket full up, of "If I had my life to live over, I would have found you sooner so I could love you longer"? In reality, "A perfect marriage," as someone has suggested, "is just two imperfect people who refuse to give up on each other." They make a choice to make it work and are willing to labor through the difficulties.

There are magical times and memories ingrained in our minds and hearts, but sometimes there is bad news. In reality, the world in which we live will not make it easy to sustain those exciting times over the long haul. An extra portion of significant effort and extended sacrificial love on the part of both parties is needed. Many of us have experienced the downers. It may have reached the point of feeling, "He's not the man I married," or "She's not the woman I married." If you stay with this perspective for an extended period of time, the landscape becomes filled with sadness and loneliness, and you feel as if the pilot light of your soul has gone out.

As you read through these short chapters, men may feel like it is a manual for man-bashing. Certainly, this is not intended. Nor is it intended as a guilt trip. Very simply, it is an attempt to encourage a man in the nurturing process with his wife, and through that process, it encourages a woman to provide that needed affirmation and encouragement and respect for her husband. Pointing out the pitfalls aids in understanding what causes stress in marriages for both husbands and wives. Most couples will never fully attain the total euphoric state they realized in the courtship and honeymoon stages of their relationship. They've conquered that. As the focus on their partner diminishes with time and added responsibilities, more is taken for granted. Often and inadvertently, the emotional side of the relationship lags. With a concerted effort, couples can keep the flame alive in a loving, caring companionship.

We'll look at ways for your relationship to maximize those good feelings with staying power. We'll look at the potholes and pitfalls that often throw a wrench into the best intentions, and we'll also look at ways to repair some of the hurts and heartaches, even if the relationship has a near flatline pulse and needs extensive damage control. I use quotes, illustrations, and stories along with some friendly humor to help you understand the nature of the marriage relationship. Several of the quotes and illustrations are things I have picked up over time and are from sources unknown to me. Some I have made up, and some are sayings from my upbringing. In my desire to present more of the mystique of what makes marriages work, I have acknowledged known sources.

This book is not intended to be an exhaustive, in-depth study on marriage, but rather some common sense, practical, and helpful insights into strengthening your partnership. It is intended to help you realize, as a couple, that there is often a need to do something to make things better. You might call it a wake-up call. Follow-up resources are listed in the back of the book. I also encourage you to consider coaching from a professional therapist to provide specialized help as you seek to experience a more enjoyable relationship with your partner.

Hopefully, you will find this short, simple book to be encouraging and affirming. If your relationship has gone off the rails, my desire is that you will find encouragement as you rebuild and re-bond. Hope really is a confidence that things will work out, for all things are possible if you believe and if you are willing to try. The achievement of your goal of a loving, caring, lasting relationship is assured the moment both partners commit themselves to make it happen. May this book provide you with the inspiration and encouragement to give it your very best effort and so prove that hope truly is a powerful ally.

Let Love Go Forward
. . . from this time and place

Terry Olsen
Kenmore, Washington

CHAPTER 1

Living Happily Ever After

If I could live my life over again . . . Next time I would find you sooner so I could love you longer.
—Kaceem Madridista

Coming out of our neighborhood Safeway store with a bouquet of beautiful flowers in my hand, I happened upon a friend. The usual greeting: "Hi, how are you?"

The usual response: "Fine, how are you doing?"

Then he asked me, "Hey, why the flowers? Birthday? Anniversary?" Then jokingly he added, "Or is she mad at you for something?"

We had a good laugh. (He must have seen the sign on a floral shop marquee several miles down the road that read, "Take your wife some flowers. She must be mad at you for something.")

"No," I answered, "just a surprise for my wife."

He acted a bit amazed and asked if I did this often.

"Now and then," I said. "Just a little something to let her know she is special to me and that I love her very much." I also added that my wife is my hero, and it is important to me to let her know that. I told him I found as much joy in giving the flowers to her as she did in receiving them.

I may have perplexed his entire afternoon as he tried to take in our encounter. He's married now. Frankly, I hope that if he remembers our conversation, his wife will also be surprised, and for that special moment, feel affirmed and appreciated by her husband.

We're talking about one simple act of kindness that can be worth a hundredfold when it comes to nurturing a marriage. It can truly be part of, "And they loved happily ever after."

When we say "happily ever after," we have to stop and realistically add, "Whoa, not so fast." As we know, not all of our marriages go on in a fairy-tale way. In fact, most have their rough edges along with some big bumps on the journey. We might see a couple that seems to be in a perfect marriage, but most likely they would tell you they have had some difficult times and have had to work through their differences.

I fall into the category of those who had high hopes of a long-term marriage when I said "I do" to a beautiful, young, and gifted woman. The problem came when I had no idea what marriage entailed—not a clue! I thought I did. There was the courtship process, otherwise known as *the chase*, the wedding, and then I was to get busy in my job supporting her and our eventual children. It seemed like I was a good guy doing my best. Wow, did I ever miss it!

I surely don't want to lead you astray lest you think that because I had a bouquet of flowers I was some sort of super husband. I had no idea what the word *relationship* meant, nor the word *nurture*. Nurture? What in the world is that? Maybe another word for nurture would be *cultivate*. Nurturing is a process of cultivation. Neither of those words were part of my marriage vocabulary. I did not have a clue. Something about us men—we just don't get it.

Not Having a Clue

Let me fill you in. After twelve years and two children, in a marriage in which my wife made a good attempt at making it work, I became a divorce statistic. I was too closed-minded to think it could end. Truth is, I was busy in my work with a Christian outreach to high school students. My wife was very patient with my efforts, but I did not realize I was giving her the leftovers of my time. Of course, she couldn't feel like she was important to me when I was working during the day and speaking at least two nights a week and on occasional weekends. When I was home, there were the needs of keeping a home going (cleaning, yard work, grocery shopping, working in the garage—anything where I didn't have to deal with any "problems.") Let's call these things diversions. There were also the needs of two young children, something she had been balancing every day, plus working a job. She was an excellent schoolteacher and busy in her work. How could I be so blind as not to see we were slowly drifting apart? You might say we were two good, decent people passing like ships in the night. I was totally unaware of what building a friendship with my wife was all about, and I was unintentionally participating big-time in a soon-to-be-broken relationship.

Unfortunately, I was motoring along unaware that she was sinking into emotional despair as I was fully engrossed in my work. Not being any kind of a nurturer, I didn't even pick up on her feelings. She would often remind me that we should take some time to talk. Typically, we men want to get things fixed quickly and move on.

> You might say we were two good, decent people passing like ships in the night.

Here is an illustration of what I mean:

The husband arrives home from work, and after greeting his wife with a kiss, she says, "Honey, we need to talk." At which point he says, "What's there to talk about? The washer and dryer work, don't they?"

That is a simple illustration, but it shows that husband and wife are not even on the same page. Men have this thing about getting it fixed and moving on. Of course, I fit the mold. Truth be told, most men suffer from the impression they can fix anything, including a struggling marriage. My now ex-wife also suggested counseling, which of course, I didn't feel we needed since we men feel we can fix things. Why pay good money when we can figure this thing out? (Interestingly, I later went back to school to earn another degree, and I did marriage and family counseling for a number of years.) My belief today is that every person can benefit from talking with a professional therapist, especially during a stressful period in life. A good therapist can become a coach and help set a game plan for resolution and success.

Finally, after a few attempts to make things work, we came to understand it wasn't going to be "happily ever after," and a divorce ensued. I wasn't really willing to make changes. Looking back, I have to say I cannot blame her. Knowing what I know now, I take full responsibility. In hindsight, I was just too wrapped up in my work. I have amusingly said, "I was getting myself confused with the second person of the Trinity." I was not the Savior for the high school kids I was working with. That was the Lord's doing. Our "for better or for worse" ended up for worse. What had started out so promising with good chemistry during the chase ended with her feeling, "I don't need this anymore" and "He's not the man I married." Perhaps some of you are experiencing this same story. Most likely, one of you is crying out loud for help. I hope the cry is not going unheeded.

Length of Time in Marriages

In researching information for this book, I came across several different opinions on the time periods when marriages are truly tested. They either operate within a healthy give-and-take or simply dissolve into a divorce. I list the following as the years of marriage when breakdowns tend to occur.[1]

One to two years:

This is a time of adjustment when two singles are blending into one couple. Not always an easy task, often coming from different upbringings, belief systems, work ethics, possibly bringing children into a second marriage, or significant differences trying to meld into one new system. Often both partners are working and going separate ways. When the chase is over, men often forget the courting/nurturing process that brought them the prize.

Five to seven years:

There are more responsibilities, possibly a new home. Often by this time there is a first child. Usually, more responsibilities come with each job. Then comes possible financial stress if "wants" outpace "needs."

Ten to thirteen years:

Though studies say the average length of marriage is around eight years, my observation is that the usual breakdown is in the ten-to-thirteen-year range. A second child has arrived. There are more responsibilities at home and work. Children's activities make for a harried day with soccer, little league, music and swim lessons, and medical appointments. Then come the unexpected things out of our control: sickness, a broken arm when a kid falls out of a tree, appliance malfunction, traffic jams, inclement weather, etc. A chopped-up daily routine creates stress, and physical health can suffer. People often wear themselves down with all their work and activities. The corporate ladder is enticing because both parents want to move up. Perhaps there is a push for a new home with more space, which could add more financial stress. They are not taking enough time with each other; they are forgetting those things that made good chemistry in earlier days.

Nineteen to twenty-one years: Kids have their own activities. They are old enough to do things for themselves, which can mean they don't always want Mom and Dad around. Both parents have many activities, including kids' school activities. Sometimes the corporate ladder is still calling. Some other person may appear attractive and draw interest. Affairs get started this way. Some men still think they have what it takes to make another woman "happy" if they feel their own needs are not being met. Is this another chase? Some women may feel they are starving for intimacy and begin flirting, which can also easily lead to an affair.

No matter the length of a marriage, no one likes a broken relationship. Nobody wins, and the emotional toll is so hurtful and debilitating, often with frustration, anger, and bitterness. Children feel the emotional sting, sometimes taking a responsibility that is not rightfully theirs. We would all love to experience the "happily ever after." Many couples do, and most likely they have had to work through some differences.

A Good "Ever After" Story

Here is a story that truly falls into the "ever after" category, the envy of every married person. An elderly man in his eighties hurried to his 8:00 a.m. doctor appointment.

He wanted to finish quickly because he had to be somewhere else in one hour. The doctor asked what the next appointment was. He proudly said that he went to the assisted-living facility every morning to eat breakfast with his wife at 9:00 a.m.. The doctor asked about his wife's condition. The man said that his wife had Alzheimer's disease, and for the past five years, she hasn't known who he is. The surprised doctor asked the man why he continues to go faithfully if she has no idea who he is. The old man replied, "Because I still know who *she* is." This, my friend, is real love. We should all be so lucky to have this kind of spouse. Talk about commitment! This is living happily ever after, even when the times are tougher than we'd like.

Going Forward

Get your cup of coffee or hot chocolate and sit down at the kitchen table after the kids have been tucked in. Time to have a chat.

Going back to the beginning, what do you remember most about your parents and their marriage? What color would you use to describe it and why (i.e., red = anger; blue = gloom, dull; yellow = happy, bright; brown = industrious, always working; green = adventurous; pastel color = full of life; etc.)?

Throughout your elementary school years, what do you remember as happy and unhappy times for you within your family?

What positives from your parents' marriage do you feel you brought to your marriage? What negatives did you observe from their marriage that you did not want to bring to your marriage? How has that worked out for you?

CHAPTER 2

The Chase

To the world you may be one person; but to
one person you may be the world.
—Dr. Seuss

In Paris, France, the authorities were recently concerned about one of their bridges becoming too heavy. It wasn't because of traffic or heavily laden trucks. It was because of a long-standing tradition called Locks of Love.[2] Perhaps you have heard about this. It seems that young couples who are romantically inclined choose a padlock, and both parties inscribe their names on the lock. Then on a planned outing, probably on a moonlit night, the couple clamps the lock onto a part of the bridge, thus signifying their undying love for each other. So many locks have been placed on the bridge over the years that Parisian authorities have concluded the bridge is now holding too much weight along with the cars and trucks, and they have banned the practice of love locks. To the chagrin of many young lovers, the authorities have begun to cut the love locks off. Incidentally, this is not only being done in France; there are love locks being clamped to other bridge cables, screens, railings, statues, etc. in Sweden, Russia, Germany, South Korea, China, and other countries as lovers lock their souls together in a forever bond.[3]

Needs and Faults

So the quest for the perfect love relationship blooms in many ways. In my day, we referred to it as the courtship process. Today, it is often referred to as hanging out. For this book, we'll call it *the chase*. Using stick figures, let me explain how the chase works.

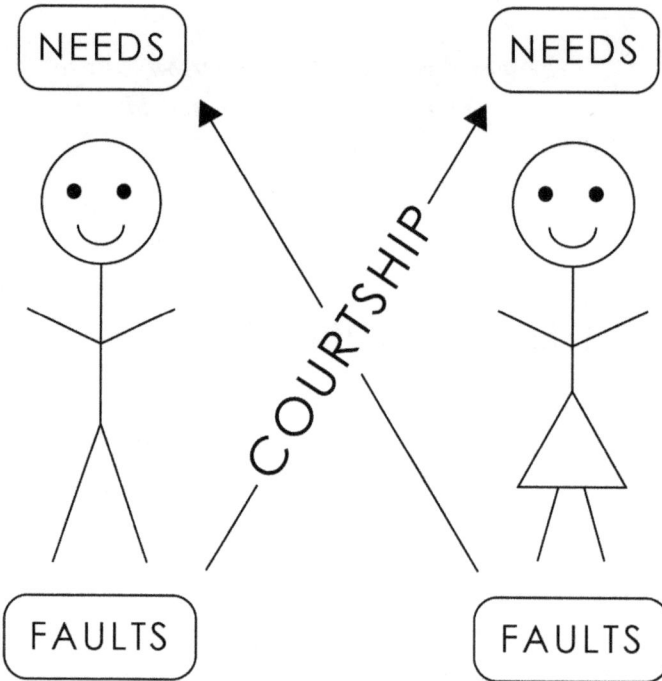

When a man sees someone he is interested in, he thinks in terms of reaching out to her. He will do this with phone calls, flowers, an occasional note, asking for a date, a short stop by at work to say hello, etc. If she is not interested, she will try to convey that by telling him so or by mostly ignoring him. As you can see with our stick characters, we all have our needs and faults. In reaching out, the man (usually the pursuer) wants to downplay his faults and attempt to meet the woman's needs at the same time. Often those needs are for affirmation and encouragement, thus his attempt to show his caring interest. In turn, the woman attempts to minimize her faults and to be interested in his needs. If there is interest, she may reach out with an occasional phone call, a note card, or maybe some cookies she baked, to meet some of his needs so that he might feel he is valued.

As you can see, the line drawn between the faults (which both parties work to keep at a minimum) goes to meeting the needs of the other party. This line we will call the courtship process, as expressed in the arrows going away from one's faults and toward the other's needs. As the man and woman's friendship grows, they will reach out in other ways to affirm and encourage each other. (And, by the way, each party will usually work to reduce the faults they see in their own life.)

Finding "Perfection"

This goes along for some time; the chemistry, camaraderie, and bonding grow, and they decide to say, "I do." They have found the perfect one they have been "chasing." The woman feels she has found her man of steel; he is committed, caring, and courageous, having character, integrity, kindness, consistency, and patience. This guy has it all.

The man feels as if he has found the first bloom of spring, every bit the beautiful, spectacular rose; she is caring, considerate, communicative, creative, kind, and every other positive adjective that comes to mind.

In time they will discover that the right brain/left brain debate enters the picture. You may have heard of it. For the most part, man is considered the left-brainer—analytical, practical, logical, rational, get it fixed and move on, prone to punctuality as it pertains to his job, disciplined in his thinking, getting it right, no excuses, often inconvenienced with children's needs, and usually, most men have a hard time with changes. A simple illustration points this out. The woman rearranges the furniture in the living room, and when the husband walks through the door, his comment is usually not, "Honey, this looks really nice." It is often, "Why did you change that?" A man is typically less tied into the emotional and creative side, though some men seem to have been gifted with, or have figured out, right-brain tendencies.

The woman is usually regarded as a right-brainer—the one who is creative, more easily emotional, wanting to talk it over, seeming to be more caring, often more patient and calm, and often not too rattled by inconvenience. Women are often more open to trying different things and are seemingly more understanding of emotional needs in adults and children.

The Best-Laid Plans

As the years go by, both partners realize that the stick illustration doesn't always reflect reality. Patterns are built, and some are not always positive. (More on this in a later chapter.) Instead of seeking to meet the other person's needs, one or both may reverse the stick illustration and not be meeting the other's needs, but are looking at their partner's faults. And not just looking at their faults, but focusing on their faults. As time goes on, a tendency builds to accept the faults and forget about meeting the other person's needs. This, of course, can only lead to distance in the relationship. Looking at the stick people now, you will notice that the arrows are moving *toward* the faults from both parties. Hence, the woman feels, "This is not the man I thought I was marrying." And the man feels, "This is not the woman I thought I was marrying."

So the big chase to conquer and win the favor of the woman of his dreams now begins to fade, and often there arises criticism, sometimes cynicism, and negativity comes to the forefront. Likewise, the woman

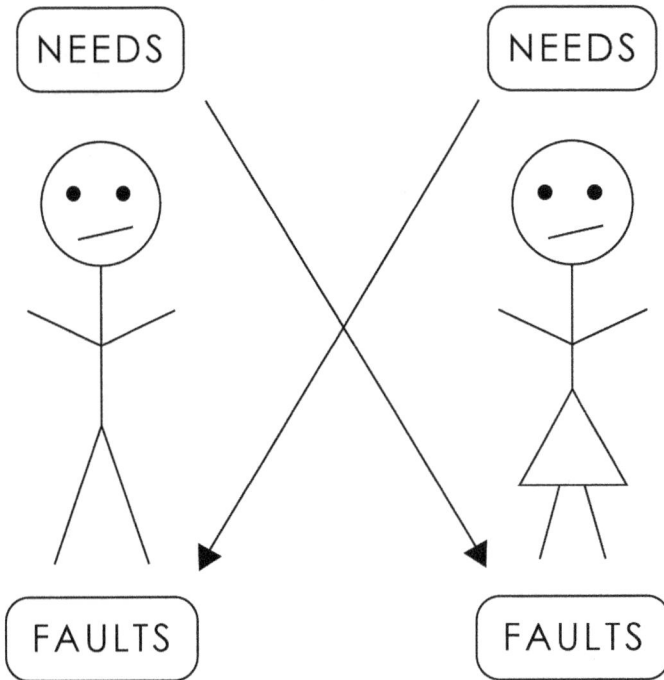

often feels his, and her, romantic dreams slipping away and those unwanted negative characteristics rising. And who likes to live in a household where these negatives abound? So why did this happen? It is because the man has unintentionally forgotten what the chase was all about—the prize he was so excited about winning earlier? He conquered and thought that was it. The battle has been won as the couple said, "I do." Unfortunately, he forgot to continue the winning formula, the courtship process. In short, he forgot to nurture his valued treasure. He forgot to do those little things, those kindnesses and courtesies, that so impressed the woman of his dreams and made her feel valued. Hence, he really isn't the man she married, so she isn't that excited to reach out to him as she did in those courtship days.

Insensitivity Sets In

Get a load of this interview between a husband and a sergeant at the police station. I think it will humorously illustrate how easy it is for men to lose focus and be totally unaware of even the simplest details about their wives.

> Husband: "My wife is missing. She went shopping yesterday and has not come home."
>
> Sergeant: "What is her height?"
>
> Husband: "Gee, I'm not sure. A little over five feet tall."
>
> Sergeant: "Weight?"
>
> Husband: "Don't know. Not slim, but not really fat."
>
> Sergeant: "Color of eyes?"
>
> Husband: "Sort of brown, I think. Never really noticed."
>
> Sergeant: "Color of hair?"
>
> Husband: "Changes a couple of times a year. Maybe dark brown now. I can't remember."
>
> Sergeant: "What was she wearing?"
>
> Husband: "Could have been pants, or maybe shorts. I don't know exactly."
>
> Sergeant: "What kind of car was she driving?"
>
> Husband: "She left in my Jeep."
>
> Sergeant: "What kind of Jeep is it?"
>
> Husband: "It's a 2010 Rubicon with Sprintex supercharger and intercooler, DiabloSport T-1000 Trinity programmer, Teraflex Falcon 3.3 shocks, 1350 RE reel drive shafts, Method 105 bead locks, Toyo 37 by 13.5 tires, custom Olympic off-road bumper, Olympic off-road Smuggler rear bumper with tire carrier, Seward radius 4s LED light, Seward 12-inch LED light bar, 50-inch LED light bar with Pod LED switch pod with Boost gage, rigid LED lights, 15-pound power tank, Rock Hard cage, Rock Hard under armor, Poison Spyder sliders,

Poison Spyder crusher fenders, 5.13 gears, Magnum 44 front axle, Cobra 75 CB radio, et cetera."

At this point the husband begins to choke up.

Sergeant: "Don't worry, buddy; we'll find your Jeep."

And so it is; the husband could barely describe any features about his wife, but by golly, he knew every detail about his Jeep. How about the sergeant's response? He doesn't seem to get it either.

When this type of insensitivity prevails, the woman no longer feels she is that important to him. She often no longer feels affirmed or appreciated. When a person's "love bucket" of appreciation and encouragement is empty, they don't have much to give. So she does the chores around the house and takes care of the kids and the pets, pretty much feeling like she is just existing, maybe even on an island of loneliness without much emotional feeling within the home. Likely, she also has a full- or part-time job, ending up each day physically and emotionally exhausted. Certainly there is not much emotional feeling for the man she married. The pleasure that was once shared in the sexual act with her husband has long since been forgotten. Now it is just a matter of satisfying his needs, taking on the form of obligation or duty, and just existing. In fact, caring for the other's needs takes a backseat as the faults rise to the forefront. Often a destructive pattern of communication ensues until, finally, what started out as two good and decent people enjoying life ends up with the people just existing together. (More on this in chapter 6.)

> When a person's "love bucket" of appreciation and encouragement is empty, they don't have much to give.

The Blame Game

Unfortunately, this often ends in some sort of blame game. I share with you a personal story from my home life. My mother and father were good people. They worked hard through the Great Depression, World War II, and the Korean conflict. I commend them for their work ethic, which was paramount. But our home was not always harmonious. Dad left home for a year at my mother's request, and they sought a divorce. I was twelve years old, the oldest son, and, of course, not sure what was going to happen. Was I to blame? Did I cause some of this? What would happen to my brothers? Children often wonder if they might be the cause.

Our mother did a good job of keeping everything together on the home front. There was much blaming between my mother and father for the separation—again, pointing to each other's faults. To my dad's credit, he was faithful to see us nearly every Sunday, usually for a ride and ice cream.

After about a year, my parents appeared in court for some sort of resolution, and the judge told them there were no grounds for a divorce. (No-fault divorce did not exist at that time.) He said, "You two go home and start working it out." Thus, Dad moved back home, and they lasted together for fifty-two years. However, I can say that it was not always harmonious. Dad was pretty much into his things: work, golf, and bowling, and our mother made sure the needs of us boys were met. Simply put, they existed under the same roof and provided for their boys. I believe my father thought he was doing the best he could in caring for my mom. He did not have a good role model. Mom just needed more of what brought them together; she needed the one who saw her as a valued person, just as in the chase.

A Flower Tells the Story

A simple illustration provides a picture of what happens within a person's mind and heart. Like a flower that closes up at night to protect against a cooler evening, so a person tends to close up when things are chilly. Distance within the relationship will prevail. As a new day dawns, that flower opens to the warmth of the sun and blooms in the brightest display of its intended color. Warmth has a way of bringing the intended beauty to the surface. So, too, with the human personality. When a person feels affirmed, appreciated, and loved, joy floods the heart and is present in a person's demeanor. You can often tell how a person is doing by reading the expression on his or her face.

When a flower stays closed for a long time and the warmth of the sun seems to pass it by on a daily, weekly, monthly, or maybe even a yearly basis, that flower may eventually bend toward sunlight and warmth in a different direction. A person's emotional needs may move him or her to seek love outside of marriage—to have an affair. Paraphrasing words from a Nina Simone song, "You learn to leave the table when you are not feeling loved."[4]

Truly, when there is a chill in the air and that flower closes up, the wonderful and accelerating chase has taken on a whole new perspective. But take heart, hang in there, as we move on through the book. We can turn those stick figures focused on the faults into something positive. Of course, *this is a choice both parties must make.* Perhaps a couple verses from "Let Love Go Forward," a song by singer and songwriter Mark Pearson, says it best:

> Love can unite us though we are apart.
> Love is the answer we all know by heart.
> Hopeful and faithful whatever we may do,
> Love now waits for us to choose.
>
> Let the light of love always shine from you,
> Illuminates what is fine and true.
> May you shine with your own special light;
> Together let us light up the night.[5]

Going Forward

Sit down at the kitchen table with a cup of coffee in hand and recount your courtship.

What were your impressions on first meeting your spouse? After the first date?

Remind each other of the times you thought were special during the courtship process: special places you went, special things you did, i.e., movies, concerts, day outings, hikes, bike rides, fairs, first kiss, etc. You might even write them down, which may remind you of other special times.

The things I remember most from our early courtship are:

CHAPTER 3

The Power of Affirmation

I can live two months on one good compliment.
—Mark Twain

One day I went to the post office as I had often done once a quarter to mail out over three hundred copies of a *Family Insights* newsletter to those on my nonprofit organization mailing list. I spoke at seminars, workshops, PTA meetings, and retreats primarily on parenting issues, and even more specifically to fathers, under the *Family Insights* banner, for eighteen years.[6] In the process of putting out this type of mailing, there are certain regulations and forms to be filled out. On occasion, the US Postal Service, in trying to update its delivery process, would upgrade the forms and the way certain zip codes were bundled. Upon my quarterly visit to the bulk-mail room, I would often encounter an older gentleman (I'll call him Ted) who was there, seemingly, just to criticize my attempts to get things correct. Usually he would let me know I had blown it again and tell me to go over to the work table and get it right.

I surmised there might possibly be something else going on in his life that was making him miserable, and my inadequacies didn't make for a very good afternoon for him. Every now and then, another postal worker would amble in and ask if they could help. I would say, "I guess I didn't get the new format correct," and they would be most willing to help. They told me Ted was often grouchy, and they'd help when they could. Of course, they had no idea when I would show up, and it seemed Ted was always there, serving out the last three years of his career with the postal service before retiring. So, as the saying goes, I would grin and bear it and be on my way.

Knowing that I was due to make another bulk mailing in a few days, I said to my wife that I just knew I was going to face Ted again. I told her I was going to try something different. I was going to bake him a pumpkin Bundt cake, wrap it up in a nice cellophane wrap with an attractive ribbon, and take it to him as a gift. (Incidentally, the recipe for this delicious cake is reprinted in the back of this book.) So, I baked it, wrapped it very nicely with clear wrap and ribbon, and headed for Ted and the US Postal Service with my bulk mailing for that quarter. I walked in with my box of letters, set them down on the work table, walked over to Ted, and handed him the nicely wrapped Bundt cake. I said, "Ted, I want to thank you for being here for me every time I have come in with my box of letters. I know you haven't felt that I knew how to get the forms done correctly, but eventually they were completed. I want you to have this gift of a pumpkin Bundt cake."

Ted was in shock. He took the cake, and tears began to roll down his cheeks. As he attempted to wipe his eyes, he looked at me and said, "Thank you so much. In all my years, no one has ever thanked me for my work here or treated me this way." The poor man was just overcome. That day I discovered the value of helping to make someone feel they were worthwhile. I will point out that every time after that when I came in with my box of bulk-mail letters, Ted greeted me with a friendly smile, called me by name, and helped me get the paperwork correct. I had no idea the effect of a simple gesture. I saw the power of affirmation in action.

Affirmation Reaches Out

So what is this thing called affirmation? Affirmation can come forth in many different ways. It may be a kind word. It may be some sort of encouragement extended to another in word or deed. It may look something like this: "You are important to me." "You are so special." "I value our friendship." "I couldn't have done it without you." "I am so proud of you." "I believe in you." "You are the best." "I appreciate all you have done." "We can always depend on you." "Let me help you with that." "Is there anything I can do to help?" I am sure you get the point; just being attentive to the other person brings encouragement. You are expressing to the other person that they are valued.

A quick look at the opposite of positive recognition will allow you to easily see what happens when we focus on the negative or on another's faults, as expressed in chapter 2. comments like, "It'll never work," "We don't have time for that," "There are better ways of doing it," "That's stupid," "It's not good enough," "Why did you do that?" or "We've never done it that way." Again, you get the point. Wowsers! That throws cold water on any sort of encouragement, and no one likes to be around negativity.

> That day I discovered the value of helping to make someone feel they were worthwhile. There are no unimportant people.

Those who study human behavior will say that every person needs to experience recognition. Every person needs to know they count—that they are valuable. There are no unimportant people. I write about this importance in my book encouraging fathers to be there for their children.[7] But as adults, we all need this too—just to know that we are valued for who we are. Affirmation brings a person's value quotient upward, which brings encouragement in the daily routine. How about this for an equation:

Attention + Affirmation + Encouragement = Positive Responses

And positive responses will produce more affirmation. Taking it a step further, when you reach out to affirm and encourage others, something happens to you. My mother had a wonderful saying that she passed on to her boys. How could we forget it? She pasted it on the mirror in our bathroom so we had to see it every day. Today it is a tape that plays in the back of my mind often: "Happiness is like a perfume. You cannot give to others without getting a few drops on yourself." For the record, my mother was the eternal optimist, and she saw the possibility of a positive outcome in even the darkest of days. She was also a realist, having lived through the Great Depression, World War II, a near divorce, and a not-so-pleasant home life. She told us once that during the Depression years, her family would sometimes put soda crackers in a bowl and pour hot water over them so they would expand, which would make it seem like there was more to eat for dinner. She was part of "the greatest generation." I cannot imagine what that would be like. She often reminded us that it was all about attitude, and we could make a choice: we could choose to see things with positive potential or we could wallow in the negative. We were reminded that no matter how bad things were, something good could always come from them. In a sense, she was telling us what Zig Ziglar years later put into words: "Always remember that your present situation is not your final destination. The best is yet to come."[8]

The Mindsets of Men and Women

Now that we have established the importance of how significant affirming another person is, let us look at what tends to occupy our mindset. Somehow we are not always programmed to think in terms of other people and what it takes to build them up. Most often we are focused on what makes our world go around. Someone has come up with a humorous pie chart of what we are most often thinking about. As you can see, men and women are not really on the same page. As you look at the two diagrams, you will no doubt experience a chuckle. (The author of this bit of humor is unknown to me.)

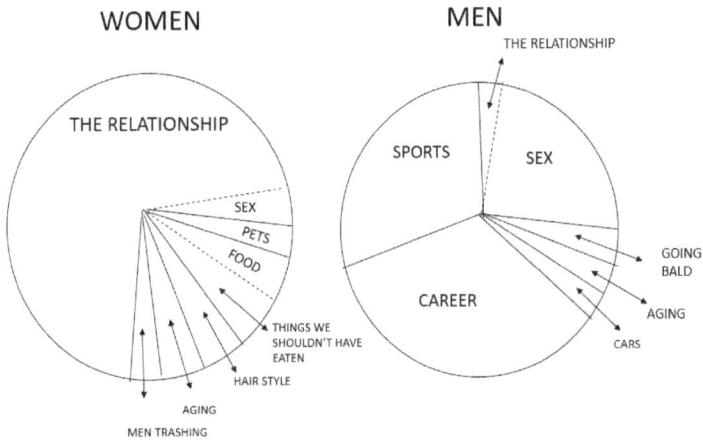

This, of course, paints with a broad brush where both men and women are coming from. Nonetheless, most people would agree that it is representative of what our thought patterns are. You will see why most men don't often think in terms of affirming their partners. Men are plugged in to three main areas in their lives. The nurturing relationship of the woman they married scarcely gets a mention, whereas from a woman's viewpoint, the relationship is paramount to everything else.

Men Don't Often Think "Affirming"

Another picture from my home life is a good illustration. In my father's later years, he was in failing health and in a convalescent center. I visited four to five times a week and occasionally took him to a Seattle Mariners game. He loved baseball. One evening as we were driving home from a ballgame, he remarked that he felt very lucky to be married to my mother. I responded, "Dad, have you told her that lately? It would be nice for her to hear it," knowing that at times the relationship at home had been a bit rocky.

He replied, "Oh, Terry, she knows that. I've told her before."

"I think she would love to hear that again, Dad," I said.

He responded, "I'm sure she knows."

Once again, guys don't often seem to be on the same wavelength as women's emotions, with the continuing need to know they are loved and valued.

Thinking back on the episode of that evening, I was reminded of the story of a couple's discussion that went something like this: The wife says, "Honey, you never tell me you love me anymore." The husband replies, "I told you when we were first married that I loved you, and if that ever changes, you'll be the first to know." So much for affirmation and encouragement. A woman needs to hear, "I love you" often.

I believe you get my drift about the power of affirmation. The positives of word and deed, of hugs and embraces, of any kind of reaching out to the other person with notes, flowers, cookies, pumpkin Bundt cake, a special surprise now and then, or even calling them by name with a smile have immense power in their effect. A proverb says it pretty well: "Gracious words are a honeycomb, sweet to the soul and healing to the bones" (Prov. 16:24). Or as the saying goes, "The more sugar, the sweeter it is."

The Value of Physical Touch

One more thing: the importance of touch. The value of a hug cannot be overemphasized. Listen to what Helen Colton, author of *The Gift of Touch*, has to say about two people hugging or touching one another:

> "The amount of hemoglobin in the blood increases significantly. Hemoglobin is a part of the blood that carries

vital supplies of oxygen to all organs in the body—including the heart and the brain. An increase of hemoglobin tones up the whole body, helps prevent diseases, and speeds up recovery from illness." Her book goes on to say, "Regular hugging can actually prolong life by curing harmful depression and stimulating a stronger will to live. The warm, meaningful embrace can have a very positive effect on people, particularly during times of widespread stress and tension- like today."[9]

Speaking of hugs, in a former book I suggested the following:

Hugs are: . . . Practically Perfect . . . Low Energy Consumption High Energy Yield . . . No Monthly Payments . . . Non-Fattening Inflation Proof . . . No Additives . . . No Preservatives Non-Taxable . . . Non-Polluting . . . Fully Refundable

To purposely belabor the point of physical touch, I give you the words of Virginia Satir, a twentieth-century psychotherapist often referred to as the pioneer of family therapy: "We need four hugs a day for survival. We need eight hugs a day for maintenance. We need twelve hugs a day for growth."[10]

On a personal note, I remember taking a bit of a risk and asking my wife, Mardi, this question: "What can I do to be the best husband I can be for you?" In asking a question like this, you never quite know what answer you might get. After some thought, she answered, "I wish you would hold me more." Ah, there it is again: the physical touch—not to have it lead to sex, but just to be held in a warm embrace.

Realizing the importance of physical touch, I share a word from the prophet Isaiah from the Scriptures. In Isaiah 40:11 we read, "He [the Lord] tends his flock like a shepherd: He gathers the lambs in his arms and carries them close to his heart." Perhaps this would be a good illustration for husbands in gathering our wives and our children in our arms and holding them close to our hearts. Do you think this might bring a strong message to them of how highly we value and cherish them? As Dr. Gary Chapman says in his book *The 5 Love Languages*, physical touch is a powerful vehicle for communicating marital love.[11]

Affirming One's Self

Throughout this chapter I have stressed the importance of affirming others. However, I want you to know that all of us need to affirm ourselves, which will provide inspiration and encouragement as we muddle through each day. I made these up when I was going through a rough stretch in my life. You might remind yourself each day of the following:

1. Thank You, Lord. You have created me, and I am special to You. (Ps. 139:13–16)
2. Thank You, Lord. You have good plans for me. (Jer. 29:11–13)
3. Thank You, Lord. You have created me for good works. (Eph. 2:10)
4. Thank You, Lord. I am in the process of becoming the person You want me to be, and the person I want to be. (Jer. 18:1–6)

There is something about finding the positive in yourself, about loving yourself, that encourages you to reach out to others. I have shared this story before, but it is so revealing. When my daughter, Megen, was five years of age, we were living in Portland, Oregon. We were preparing to visit my parents and some friends up north in Seattle, Washington. As we were getting ready to go, Megen kept herself busy finger painting at the kitchen table.

"What are you painting?" I asked. I knelt next to her to see her project.

"A picture for Jack," she said in reference to our friends whom we would be visiting.

"Oh, Megen," I said, "Jack will really like your picture. That is so nice of you."

Giving her a hug, I said, "Megen, I love you." She turned toward me and gave me a big hug and kiss. (Typical of us men, I could only visualize finger paint on the back of my shirt.)

Then I was taken aback as she asked me what I considered an amazing question:

"Dad, do you love you?"

Astonished, I thought for a moment, and then I muttered, "Well, yes, Megen. I do love me."

"Good," said Megen. "Then I know you love me." This from a five-year-old without a psychology degree; I was blown away.

"Megen," I asked, "where did you get that?"

"Well, Dad," she said, "there is a girl in our class, and she said that if you really love yourself, then you can really love other people."

At that point, Dad was a bit misty-eyed. I gave Megen another hug and said, "Megen, that was beautiful."

This five-year-old had articulated an important concept. If you first love yourself, you can reach out in love to others. And so much of being able to love yourself comes from the affirmation and encouragement you receive from others and from those times of affirming yourself as a valued person, even at times when you don't feel very special. Of course, the opposite can also be true. If you don't feel good about yourself and/or your situation, you can often reach out to others in an unkind way. So often when I see someone being rude to others in word or deed, I am pretty sure there is something else going on in their life that is providing the unpleasantness.

Part of God's Creation

In spite of how we may feel at times, let us be reminded of how special we are to the God who created us. We read in Psalm 139:13–16: "For you created my inmost being; you knit me together in my mother's womb. I praise you because I am fearfully and wonderfully made; your works are wonderful, I know that full well. My frame was not hidden from you when

I was made in the secret place. When I was woven together in the depths of the earth, your eyes saw my unformed body. All the days ordained for me were written in your book before one of them came to be." This is the deep love for you as expressed in the words of your loving heavenly Father.

Affirmation Brings Value to Others

Here is one more simple illustration of what encouragement can mean to those who receive it: Recently, Mardi and I were shopping at our local grocery store when a thirtyish young woman pulled a cartload of fresh vegetables toward a display area. Obviously, she intended to put them out in a presentable display but was just waiting for customers to rearrange them as soon she got them in place. Her name tag said "Katie" (not her real name), so I said, "Katie, thank you for putting out the vegetables for us customers. I'm sure it gets frustrating from time to time to see customers handle and often toss aside your careful display. I just want you to know we appreciate your efforts to stock the vegetables for us, so thank you."

She looked at Mardi and me and said, "That is so nice of you. No one ever thanks us for doing our job. You made my day."

Those two words, *thank you*, can make a world of difference and brighten someone's day. Truly, they are affirmation words that encourage others.

I finish this chapter with another quote given to me in earlier times. This will fully reflect this whole idea of affirmation, not just to those outside the family, but it will be even more special for those we live with. "I shall pass through this world but once. Any good that I can do, or any kindness that I can show, to any human being, let me do it now. Let me not defer, nor neglect it, for I shall not pass this way again."[12] A good reminder—there are no unimportant people. God has breathed the breath of life into every person, and every person needs to know they are valued.

Going Forward

Can you remember a time earlier in your life (elementary school through high school) when you felt affirmed by an adult? What did that feel like?

How do you feel you are affirming your family members today?

Today, I will affirm or encourage my spouse in the following way, just as I would have done in the courtship process:

Tomorrow, I will look for opportunities to do the same—to thank or praise my spouse.

I will ask my spouse what I can do to be the best partner I can be.

CHAPTER 4

The Value of Friendship

A friend is someone who reaches for your
hand and touches your heart.
—Author Unknown

Some time ago I attended a memorial service for a good friend. Speaker after speaker referred to the deceased as a friend in several ways. "He was my best friend," one said. Others followed suit: "He was my good friend" and "He was a great friend." Still another, "He was one of my best friends."

Wow! To have people express their gratitude for one's friendship in such a way must have meant that the deceased was truly one of those who reached out to others. A friend does that. In most cases, that is how your relationship began with your spouse: one asking the other out for coffee at the closest Starbucks, or for a nice dinner, or a day at the beach. Thus the friendship, though embryonic, began to grow. More times together deepened more feelings of belonging, even to the point of bonding and referring to the other as "my boyfriend" or "my girlfriend"—and thus, the courtship process. It led to good times, laughable times, times of misunderstanding and making up. All the while, the roots of a positive friendship were taking hold. You could laugh at things like the saying, "A friend is someone who thinks you're a good egg, even if you are slightly cracked or sometimes slightly scrambled." Funny times added spice as well as constructive dialogue. And you began to refer to your partner as "my best friend."

As time goes by, thoughts turn more serious. The words "I love you" are more often heard as a deepening bond takes place. So what does "I love you" really mean? "I care about you"? "I'm committed to you"? "You are my one and only"? ". . . 'til death us do part"? Well, we haven't quite got that far yet.

It's Greek to Me

In the Greek culture, they had different words to mean *love* that expressed exactly what the person who spoke it was thinking. Use of the word *phileo* (pronounced phil-ay-oh) meant a friendship type of love. When you told a person you loved them using some form of this word, they understood that you loved them as a friend. (Think of the word *phileo* as in the word *Philadelphia*, the city of brotherly love.) So if you were departing the company of a friend, you might give them a hug and say, "I love you," as in, "I love you as my friend".

Another Greek word for love is *eros* (air-ross). (Think of the word *erotica*.) This means a romantic type of love. Lovers often used this word to express their romantic love for each other. I would hope that the word *phileo* would also figure very strongly in this relationship.

A third Greek word is *storge* (store-gee); it is the love within the family and extended family. A loving, caring family is strong medicine for stressful times, both without and within the family. Siblings will tangle and mix it up from time to time, but a strong bond of love (*storge*) will carry the day.

A fourth Greek word that exemplifies the strongest word for love is *agape* (awe-gaw-pay). This is a self-sacrificing love. Here is an example of agape love in its simplest form, sacrificially caring about another person: In the days when an ice cream sundae cost much less, a ten-year-old boy entered a hotel coffee shop and sat at a table. A waitress put a glass of water in front of him and asked what she could get him.

"How much is an ice cream sundae?" he asked.

"Fifty cents," replied the waitress.

The little boy pulled some coins from his pocket and studied them. "Well, how much is a plain dish of ice cream?"

By now more people were coming into the coffee shop and waiting for a table.

"Thirty-five cents," she brusquely replied.

The little boy again counted his coins. "I'll have the plain ice cream," he said.

The waitress brought the ice cream, put the bill on the table, and walked away. The boy finished the ice cream, paid the cashier, and left. When the waitress came back, she began to cry as she wiped down the table. Placed beside the empty dish were two nickels and five pennies. You see, he surmised he couldn't have the sundae because he had to have enough left to leave a tip. That is a very simple story of sacrificing for someone else.

The Ultimate Agape

Of course, the ultimate in agape love is Jesus Christ. We see this in the example of Jesus dying on the cross for the sins of individuals and for the sins of the world. The Scripture says, "The law requires that nearly everything be cleansed with blood, and without the shedding of blood there is no forgiveness" (Heb. 9:22). (More about forgiveness in a later chapter.) His agape love was a supreme sacrifice, the laying down of His life.

It is also seen in marriage where one person will often sacrifice for the needs of the other. I think of the person who becomes a caregiver when a serious illness incapacitates a mate. Out of sacrificial love, the caregivers give up many of their former pursuits. I had a wonderful friend who was retired and played golf often during the week. Once his wife became bedridden, the golf clubs stayed in the garage so he could tend to her needs, so strong was his commitment to her. That is *agape* love; that is *phileo* love; that is *storge* love. They were lovers, even if *eros* love didn't figure in at this stage in life. They endured together until "death us do part." A strong family relationship will exhibit all these forms of love, especially as family friendships are built.

Time Together Builds Friendships

In friendship there are those good times in which so many positive memories are built. There are also some rough times, which also build memories, often unpleasant. Either way, time has a way of building friendship. Think for a moment: in those early days you couldn't wait to have time with your favorite person. Also, time is the one thing that will work against you as your journey in life moves along. Without spending time together, the relationship becomes one of just existing. I know the argument of "We're just too busy." Yet I have never heard any person say, "I should have spent more time at the office." Remember from chapter 1 that my wife and I were busy people, and remember what happened as

> Without spending time together, the relationship becomes one of just existing. Doing things together is the best way to build and maintain a lasting friendship.

we just co-existed together. I know the excuses: the job, the kids, the activities, the social life, friends, etc. Remember that I said we ended up like "two good, decent people passing like ships in the night." Small wonder that a lasting friendship didn't really develop. Doing things together is the best way to build and maintain a lasting friendship. Two people going off in opposite directions just won't do it.

I know a couple who are both very busy, yet they take time to go for an evening walk together several times a week. They talk about their lives: about their highlights and lowlights of the day, about their kids, about coming events, about their vocations, and about future plans. Even if you have small children, strollers have wheels, kids can bundle up if there is cold weather, and dogs can be put on a leash. Time together is very significant in impacting a growing friendship that is the foundation for the long haul in a marriage. And lest we forget, walking is a good form of exercise.

Sometimes our friendship can bring out something laughable, as evidenced by the goof in a church bulletin about a wedding. The wedding was Saturday evening, and in the Sunday morning church bulletin were the following congratulatory words: "This past Saturday evening, our church hosted the wedding of Sarah Johanson and Sam Nelson, a lovely couple. Thus ended two years of a wonderful friendship." Obviously, it was a humorous slip by whoever does the Sunday morning bulletins. He or she probably meant to say that their wonderful friendship continues or something to that effect.

As you take time to look back over the building of your marital friendship, I share with you this poem by author Edgar Guest, most likely dedicated to a special friendship. If it doesn't fit for you at the moment, visualize a few years out and hopefully, it will fit at that time.

I'd like to be the sort of friend that you have been to me;
I'd like to be the help that you've been always glad to be;

I'd like to mean as much to you each minute of the day
As you have meant, old friend of mine, to me along the way.

I'd like to do the big things and the splendid things for you,
To brush the gray out of your skies and leave them only blue;
I'd like to say the kindly things that I so oft have heard,
And feel that I could rouse your soul the way that mine
you've stirred.

I'd like to give you back the joy that you have given me,
Yet that were wishing you a need I hope will never be;
I'd like to make you feel as rich as I, who travel on
Undaunted in the darkest hours with you to lean upon.

I'm wishing at this Christmas time that I could but repay
A portion of the gladness that you've strewn along the way;
And could I have one wish this year, this only would it be:
I'd like to be the sort of friend that you have been to me.[13]

You cannot go wrong if you base your marriage foundation on a caring friendship. That doesn't mean you won't have a hiccup or two along the way. Caring friends have a way of working through their difficulties, resulting in positive resolutions. I finish this chapter with a note on friendship taken from a Hallmark card, and also a quote from a favorite friend of children.

Friendship is . . .
. . . One of the most treasured gifts in life, given from one person to another.
. . . High praise for the one who receives it.
. . . A gift all admire and long to experience.
. . . Essential to a life lived well.
. . . Often as elusive as it is essential.[14]

"Friendship," said Christopher Robin, "is a very comforting thing to have."[15]

—A. A. Milne, *Winnie the Pooh*

Going Forward

Time for a little brainstorming over that cup of coffee. What are several things we could do *together*? Here are some suggestions: take a morning or evening walk, go grocery shopping, take the kids to the playground, walk the dog, visit an older, lonely relative, volunteer in your church or some charity, such as a food bank that would take you outside of yourselves once a week or once a month.

From our discussion, we could do the following:

Do your research on times and availability, put it on your calendar, and follow through.

CHAPTER 5

Attitude and Forgiveness

As water reflects a face, so a man's heart reflects the man.
—Proverbs 27:19

Several years ago I saw a television interview with an older couple. They had married in their late teens and were celebrating seventy years of marriage, which is somewhat remarkable by today's standards. The interviewer asked them to relate the secret of their long and happy married life. The old gentleman smiled at his wife, cleared his throat, and in a rather raspy, gravelly voice said, "It can be summed up in one word: forgiveness."

The program's host was a bit taken aback and responded, "That is it, one word?"

The gentleman replied, "Yes, that is it: forgiveness."

The power of that one word, *forgiveness*, when it is properly put forth, can bring a whole new dimension to the relationship. This is one of those attitudes in our journey that can be life-changing for both the giver and the receiver. Perhaps these words best sums it up: Failing to forgive does not make you strong; it eventually makes you bitter. Being willing to forgive, does not make you weak; it sets you free. Once you acknowledge forgiveness, you need to move on. Unfortunately, some people say they forgive, but then they forget to forgive what they say they forgave. The choice is ours. Let's take a look at the dynamics of what is involved here.

Life is going to throw us curve balls. In psychological terms, let us refer to them as stressors. Those are the times when we feel the pressure of keeping things together—the job, the kids, activities, friendships, finances, assignments, deadlines, hurtful words or deeds from others, etc. Sometimes we are not very careful with our choice of words. All of this can lead us to exclaim, "Stop the world; I want to get off!"

Maybe you have heard the old line repeated when things didn't seem to be going well: "Cheer up; things could be worse." Well, I cheered up and guess what? Things got worse. If we're not careful, all we see is negative, and we miss being thankful for all the good things in life. Even when things don't seem right, we can choose an attitude that good can come from what is now happening.

In the New Testament, James has some words for us: "Count it all joy, my brethren, when you meet various trials, for you know that the testing of your faith produces

> Failing to forgive does not make you strong; it eventually makes you bitter. Being willing to forgive does not make you weak. It sets you free.

steadfastness" (James 1:2–3 RSV). I'll admit, it is pretty tough to be joyful when life is full of struggles. As Erma Bombeck said in one of her books, "If life is a bowl of cherries, what am I doing here in the pits?"[16]

In the book of Hebrews we read, "Now faith is the assurance of things hoped for, the conviction of things not seen" (Heb.

11:1 RSV). Also, the apostle Paul reminds us, "And hope does not disappoint us, because God has poured out his love into our hearts by the Holy Spirit, whom he has given us" (Rom. 5:5). Remember, I said in my introduction to this book that hope is a powerful ally. Hope also means we take some action to deal with our situation. It may mean serious confrontation and dialogue; it may mean visiting with a professional therapist to help us work through the rough spots.

Attitude Is a Choice

In the end, it is an attitude choice we make each day, maybe each hour for some of us. That's not to say we bury our heads in the sand, submerge our feelings, and be dishonest with ourselves, hoping all the bad will go away. But it is to remind ourselves, "Your present situation is not your final destination."

Charles Swindoll, noted pastor, author, and former president of Dallas Theological Seminary, has a nice piece about attitude:

> The longer I live, the more I realize the impact of attitude on life. Attitude, to me, is more important than facts. It is more important than the past, than education, than money, than circumstances, than failures, than successes, than what other people think or say or do. It is more important than appearance, giftedness, or skill. It will make or break a company . . . a church . . . a home. The remarkable thing is we have a choice every day regarding the attitude we will embrace for that day . . . . We cannot change the inevitable. The only thing we can do is play on the one string we have, and that is our attitude . . . I am convinced that life is 10 percent what happens to me and 90 percent how I react to it. And so, it is with you . . . we are in charge of our Attitudes.[17]

The Power of Forgiveness

Recognizing that a proper attitude is paramount in relationships, let us now look at the role of attitude in the act of forgiveness. Perhaps these two topics could have been two separate chapters, but I have chosen to combine them since in many ways, they intersect. Anytime you have a negative attitude and an unforgiving spirit, you will find distance, disappointment, and even despair. One way we must respond to disappointment in our relationship is through the power of forgiveness. Just as hope is a powerful ally, so also is the attitude of forgiveness.

Recognizing that our mates cannot or do not meet all of our physical and/or emotion needs, we may often entertain some sort of feeling against a slight, whether it be a word or deed. Something may be said or done that seems out of line. Often we choose not to deal with it, so we bury it and choose to live with the lack of forgiveness. Hence, our attitude sours, leading to an unhealthy distance between partners. Carrying a grudge will only bring more distance as one partner looks at the other's faults rather than seeking to meet their needs as you saw with our stick characters in a previous chapter. Eventually, a grudge will produce negativity, cynicism, and criticisms toward the other person, and isn't that fun to live with?

Asking for Forgiveness

When we realize that there is an unhealthy attitude and/or the lack of a forgiving spirit, one or both parties need to step up and ask for forgiveness. How to ask for forgiveness? See if this approach will work for you, or you could use something similar that you would feel comfortable with. How about if you would say to your partner:

> "I have come to realize I was wrong when I said
> _____ (or when I did
> _____), and I want to ask for your forgiveness."

Or, something like this:

"I have come to realize what I said was hurtful to you, and I want to ask for your forgiveness."

It may take a while for your words to sink in if they come out of the blue and the other individual has been emotionally wounded, especially over a period of time. Remember, most men want things fixed right away. Men, it just doesn't always happen that way. Give the other person time to process what you are asking for and for the slow healing to take place. Time, and your future actions, will be on your side as you

> The stressful times handled in a correct way, with the right attitude of forgiveness, will be the foundation of a growing and lasting friendship and even good health.

continue to return to the things that brought you together in the first place: *kindnesses, courtesies*, and *encouraging words*.

Two people living together will inevitably have differences. No journey is perfect. You know the saying, "The best-laid plans . . ." It is the attitude we choose to embrace that will see us through, and our attitude is the one thing we can choose to control, no matter what the circumstances are. The good times will take care of themselves, and we take them to the bank of our good memories. The stressful times handled in a correct way, with the right attitude of forgiveness, will be the foundation of a growing and lasting friendship and even good health. It also helps us to have a positive perspective of wanting to meet the other person's needs rather than focusing on their faults. Both parties benefit when forgiveness is in play.

There may be many times when you and your partner don't agree on something, which may mean you just see things from different perspectives. You don't have to be right, nor do unkind words need to come into play. Thus, no need for forgiveness, just a gentle agreement to see things differently. Mardi and I occasionally will see the same thing and come to different conclusions. Let me give you an illustration. For several years we would vacation with five other families at Lake Chelan in north central Washington. While driving there you had to travel over the mountain pass, and on one occasion a deer passed closely in front of our vehicle. As we told the story, Mardi saw the deer as coming down the mountain, across the road, jumping the guardrail, and heading down the other side, probably toward a valley stream. When I told the story, I was sure the deer had come up the valley, jumped the guardrail, crossed the highway, and was headed up the mountain for higher ground. To this day, we both are sure we saw it as we proclaimed. Just two people who saw things differently.

That is hardly anything to get upset about, and yet there are some folks who would take a stance about something like this so adamantly it could produce distance in a relationship. They are determined that their view is the right one. You won't build a lasting relationship if you must always have the last word, nor will it produce the quality of a positive attitude about life.

A caring friend to many in her lifetime, Mother Teresa saw these words and and liked them so much she hung them in her children's home in Calcutta:

> People are often unreasonable, illogical, and self-centered. Forgive them anyway. If you are kind, people may accuse you of ulterior motives. Be kind anyway. If you are honest, people may cheat you. Be honest anyway. If you find happiness, people may be jealous. Be happy anyway. The good you do today may be forgotten tomorrow. Do good anyway. Give the world the best you have, and it may never be good enough. Give your best anyway. For you see, in the end it is between you and God. It was never between you and them anyway.[18]

I concur. It is ultimately between you and God. But also, in a marriage relationship, attitude and forgiveness involves you *and* your partner.

I finish this chapter with a thought on attitude from the book, *There's a Lot More to Health than Not Being Sick.* Former pastor and author, the late Bruce Larson tells the story of visiting a lodge for disturbed folks, and over the mantle above the fireplace was this saying: "Do you want to be right or well?"[19] For this chapter ending I changed a few words: "Do you *have* to be right, or do you *want* to be well?"

Going Forward

For the cup-of-coffee discussion, reread Charles Swindoll's words regarding attitude found about halfway through this chapter. What two or three things do you learn from his words? How does this apply to your life?

Today I will choose to make this attitude (cheerful, joyous, grateful, happy, appreciative, hopeful, affirming others) a part of my life:

What do you think keeps most people from asking for forgiveness from another person? Is there anyone within your family or outside the family whom you need to ask for forgiveness for an unkind word, attitude, or deed?

CHAPTER 6

The Big Picture

Being happy doesn't mean everything is perfect. It means you have decided to look beyond the imperfections.
—Gerard Way, musician

The day was bright and sunny as people began gathering for *the event.* The momentous occasion was ready to be celebrated. Whether in a beautiful church setting or in an outdoor, woodsy, just-as-beautiful venue, the bride and groom say their vows and walk down the aisle to the delight of those who have come to this celebration. It is a time of great joy, and it should be.

The marriage covenant is a commitment by two people who are saying their vows "before God and these witnesses" for a lifelong journey. I use the word *covenant* rather than the word *contract.* A contract can often be broken and has an "out," as they say. Yes, it is binding, but though there are often penalties, one can exit. A covenant before God with an oath to each other is much more lasting. It is referred to as establishing a bond where two parties are bound together, much as God made covenants with His people.

The marriage covenant adds a significant dimension—God, the God who breathed the breath of life into each individual. As the author of Ecclesiastes, Solomon, penned, "A cord of three strands is not quickly broken" (Eccl. 4:12). In a marriage covenant, there is a spiritual dimension that binds two souls into one flesh, a loving relationship that says, "I belong to you forever," and a prayer to the sovereign Lord to bless a lasting friendship. You would pick this up at the marriage ceremony itself when the officiant begins, "Dearly beloved" [or "Dear friends"], we are gathered together in the presence of God and these witnesses to join together this man and this woman in holy marriage, instituted by God . . ."

Of course, in the scheme of events, there are marriages that do not always fare well, and difficult times prevail. Though not supposed to be the case, it does happen. Depending on whose statistics you select, we are told that 40 to just under 50 percent of all marriages will fail.[20]

Building Communication Patterns

As a result of the highs and the lows of a relationship, I put together a chart that will help you understand what takes place in the building of patterns of communication within a marriage. Call it the big picture.[21] These patterns express what should be happening in marriage and what often actually happens because we may begin to focus on the other person's faults rather than trying to meet their needs.

GOD
MARRIAGE
TOGETHERNESS

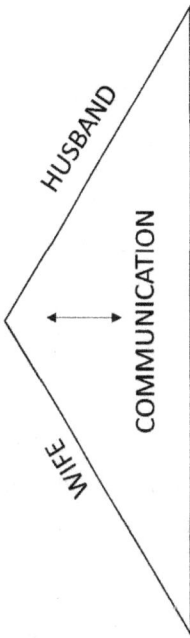

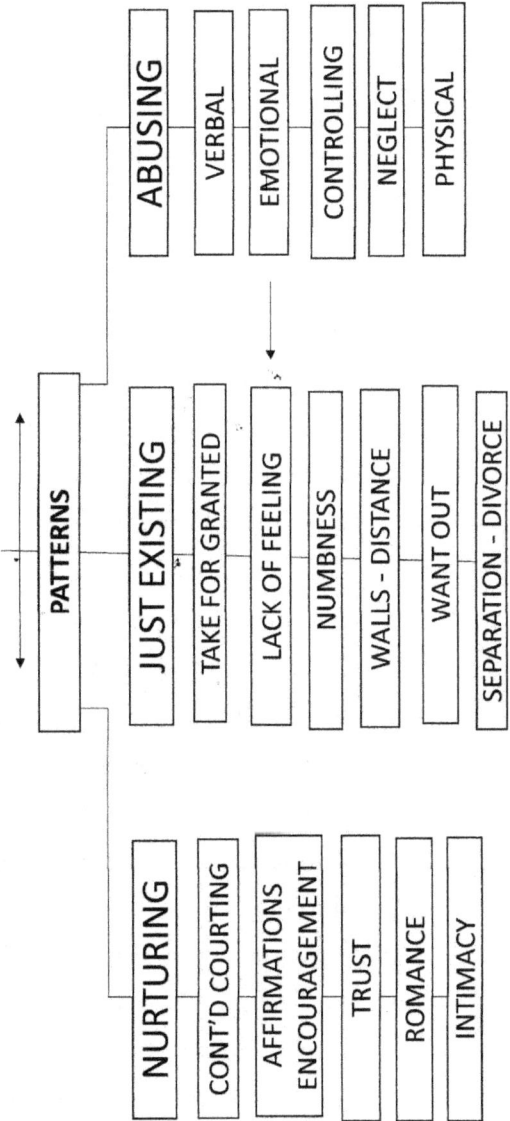

HUSBAND

WIFE

COMMUNICATION

PATTERNS

ABUSING
- VERBAL
- EMOTIONAL
- CONTROLLING
- NEGLECT
- PHYSICAL

JUST EXISTING
- TAKE FOR GRANTED
- LACK OF FEELING
- NUMBNESS
- WALLS - DISTANCE
- WANT OUT
- SEPARATION - DIVORCE

NURTURING
- CONT'D COURTING
- AFFIRMATIONS ENCOURAGEMENT
- TRUST
- ROMANCE
- INTIMACY

You will notice that the times husbands and wives will feel very close is at the apex of the triangle—often during the courtship process, the marriage ceremony, the reception, and the honeymoon. There is that sense of togetherness, the chemistry of bonding, and the feeling of great warmth in the relationship. Over time, there is still the feeling of belonging, but there is a tendency to take on different ways and means of communicating. As you can see, we may develop different patterns in our communication and feelings toward one another.

The Abusing Pattern

Unfortunately, for some couples there emerges a rather sad development. I refer to it as the abusing pattern. It is not intentional in the beginning, but over time it comes to the forefront. Most recognizable is the verbal abuse, where one party says things that are hurtful. I noticed this at times in my own family as my dad often uttered hurtful words toward my mother. This happened especially if he was inconvenienced in some way. Of course, with enough verbal abuse, the other person can feel the emotional distance and the withholding of affection and kind words. Often times, one person uses controlling manipulation, which is a form of abuse. In fact, as my friend Dr. Gregory Jantz says in his book, *Healing the Scars of Emotional Abuse*, "Any abuse is a form of control, or the fear of losing control."[22]

Another form is neglect is the silent treatment or shunning. It can be very hurtful to the one on the receiving end.

And then, of course, there is physical abuse. No one should have to put up with abuse of any kind, but especially physical abuse. All other abuses are emotionally painful, but physical abuse demands you go to the authorities to seek protection. For all abuses, it would be best to seek professional therapy for you and your partner.

A simple illustration will spell out what happens when little things are not dealt with. During the early years of the United States space program, rockets were launched from Cape Canaveral on the Florida coast. They were to be propelled down the missile range over the Atlantic Ocean. As a rocket was launched and began to soar to its hoped-for height, careful attention was paid that it was correctly on its projected course. If there was any sign near the launch that the rocket was off course, it would be immediately destroyed. Those who were monitoring its flight knew it had to be perfectly on course from the outset, or miles down the missile range it would end up far off course. That is why when something is detected out of kilter in a marriage, it is important to work at it early rather than pass it by, hoping that things will work out in time. Further down the years, things can get way out of sorts, and two good people end up distanced, disappointed, frustrated, and throwing up their hands in despair. Take the time to sort things out early on. Choose to seek a professional therapist who can act as a good coach to help you have a positive resolution.

The Nurturing Pattern

I refer to the pattern illustrated on the far left of the chart on page 65 as the nurturing pattern. Shouldn't every couple have this as a hallmark of their married life? In most cases it has been experienced in the early years of dating and marriage, but as I have explained earlier, as couples live out responsibilities over the years, the curveballs and pitfalls often lead elsewhere.

Not much explanation is needed as you look over the nurturing pattern. We have talked about the courtship process that usually left us feeling on top of the world emotionally. Then as our relationship grew over the months, we relished the affirmations and encouragement. Trust was built and romance flourished, moving to intimacy—that special place of companionship, bondedness, closeness, and belonging.

A note here to men: Being wired the way we are, we often think of intimacy as only sexual. Certainly it does mean that—a pleasure for both partners. To a woman it means more than being sexually involved. Intimacy to a woman means those things I just mentioned. Let me repeat them again: companionship, togetherness, bonding, friendship, closeness, and any other word that indicates an emotional, caring relationship. If a number of these characteristics of intimacy are missing for the woman, she is going to feel less inclined to enjoy sex with her husband.

Interestingly enough, most men don't think that way. We often think that if we are experiencing sex, everything is okay. As an added suggestion, rather than just acting on instinct, which is often centered on one's own gratification, how about making a *studied effort to understand* the honor and significance of the sexual act as it pertains to the emotions and sexual foreplay. What turns a woman on and what turns her off? Perhaps you can ask your wife to explain the difference between switching on a light bulb and heating up an iron, or ask her the difference between using a microwave and a Crock Pot as it pertains to foreplay and the sexual act. She will know the answer.

Most men do pretty well in this nurturing pursuit during the courtship process known as the chase. Occasionally someone will come to me with their marriage in shambles and ask me, "How can my relationship with my wife be better?" or "How can I save my marriage?" After some discussion as to what is going on, we eventually arrive at the following: "How about going back to those things that got you the prize in the first place?"

Then comes the puzzled, deer-in-the-headlights look, which reminds me again that most men just don't get it. After a brief explanation of what we did to win over the girl of our dreams in the first place, all of a sudden, the light goes on. You see, when we forget to take care of the treasure we sought and won, things will start going downhill. Remember the illustration of the flower in an earlier chapter? That flower needs the

> People may not remember exactly what you said or what you did, but they will never forget how you made them feel.

nurturing warmth of sunlight to bring out the most beautiful bloom. If not, it begins to close as in the coolness of night. A relationship has the same potential. It will bloom in the warmth of a caring friendship, or it will close when coolness replaces that warmth and positive nurturing is not present.

The Just-Existing Pattern

The middle pattern in our chart on page 65 is where many couples exist today. As the years roll along with jobs, kids, houses, and activities, we can drift into just existing. We begin to take each other for granted, which can only produce, in different amounts, a lack of feeling for one another. If this goes on for an extended period of time, a certain numbness enters the relationship, and then you really are just existing. Familiarity can do this. Nothing seems exciting anymore as we muddle through our daily routines. No longer attempting to consciously meet each other's needs, we soldier on with our earthly trek, sometimes resenting our position in life.

Soon there is more distance, and then emotional walls get built. Eventually, without much thought of trying to repair the hurts, anger, and frustration, one of the parties will want out—maybe a trial separation, but most likely a divorce. Everyone comes out a loser as each partner and the kids face the brokenness of the relationship. It is unfortunate because early on, with a few cracks in the foundation, the marriage could have been fixed and could have come back even stronger if both parties would have seen the value in restoring the relationship. Total brokenness leaves a hole in everyone's heart. Truth be told, most marriages have some times of testing, some little blips on the screen; others fall totally flat.

The Art of Listening

Most marriages will come back stronger if the couple has a willingness to listen carefully and hear the other person out, and then choosing to make some changes that will be beneficial to both. I should point out here that listening is looking the other person in the eye. It is turning off the TV and the cell phone and really hearing—not just what they are saying, but what they are feeling. Feelings are not necessarily right or wrong, but they are important. Feelings reflect the emotional side and are good indicators of how the relationship is going or where it is headed. That is why listening is so crucial and usually something we men must make a studied effort to do if we are going to get it right.

As I have stated, a man's first response is often to give advice so he can move on. We need to practice the art of listening and picking up on the feeling. We may have to tell our partner, "I need some help to understand what you are feeling." You may get a response that says your partner is feeling hurt, or angry, or frustrated, or confused, or sad, or depressed, or lonely, or disgusted, or anxious, etc. Whatever the response to your request, don't deny their feeling by saying, "You shouldn't feel this way." That will build a nice wall between you. How about, "I want to help. How can I best do that?" Then listen.

Any answer that seems to be directed at you in an accusing way, as in, "You always . . ." or "You never . . ." will most likely put you in a defensive position, and you will want to deny the comment. Better to say something like, "I guess I didn't realize you felt that way." That statement assures you are listening and hearing what the other person is feeling. To sum up this point: *Learn to listen. Look for the feeling.* To emphasize once again the importance of feelings, hear this statement loud and clear: "People may not remember exactly what you said or what you did, but they will never forget how you made them feel."[23] How you make others feel about themselves says a lot about you.

As the saying goes, there are three kinds of people: There are those who will listen attentively and work at changing things to make them better. There are those who will listen half-heartedly and choose to watch things unfold, which will keep everything in the just-existing mode. Finally, there are those who choose not to work at making things better and then exclaim, "What happened?" when everything totally falls apart. As you can see, there is a choice to be made when things aren't going well. Sometimes old things need to go away and better things need to be born. Sometimes marriages go through those difficult times so that new and better patterns can come forth.

Going Forward

Reread the chart with your spouse and together talk over where your marriage is. Talk about how you got where you are without pointing out blame. As Charlie Shedd recorded in his book *Letters to Philip*, the aim of discussion is not who is right and who is wrong, but the "only aim is deeper understanding."[24]

Talk about where you want to be and develop a concrete action plan to get to your goal. Most likely it will mean taking out your calendars and setting up some dates, some time to talk and reflect. All this may seem elementary, but if you want to move from the just-existing column, or even the abuse column, to the nurturing column, it will take a choice and practical planning. Remember, the present situation is not the final destination. The achievement of your goal is assured the moment you commit yourself.

CHAPTER 7

Patience and Kindness

Be kind, for everyone you meet carries a great burden.
—Ian Maclaren

"Breakfast is being served," said a friendly voice from the kitchen. Soon the family came in from different directions, taking their usual places at the antique dining room table. Dad and the three children waited patiently for the food now on its way to the table. Also on its way was the smell of something slightly burned. Toast, perhaps, or biscuits; maybe even pancakes. Those hungry kids knew it wasn't bacon; they recognized that good smell. Ah, the bottom of the biscuits had a slightly different color, like something darker had been scratched off. The kids began to grumble about the burned biscuits. Dad stepped in to remind them that burned biscuits aren't the worst thing that can happen, and with a little strawberry jam they would taste just as good as always.

As the mother went back to the kitchen to fetch something else, Dad told the children, "You know, guys, your mother works hard cooking and cleaning for us, and she works hard all week at her job outside the home. Yet she always gives us her best effort here at home. A few burned biscuits won't matter. Here is the strawberry jam."

That man was a wise father, using the incident of burned biscuits as a teachable moment. It would have been real easy to say, "Hey, how come these biscuits are burned?" or something equally demeaning, or to have allowed the kids to have voiced a burned-biscuits protest in unison. Instead, the father took the high road with praise for his wife for all her efforts for the family and reminding his children that with a little strawberry jam the biscuits would still taste good. He showed a little patience in the situation, a little kindness toward his wife, and a valuable role-model lesson for his children. In the great scheme of world events, burned biscuits are not earthshaking. How about a creative alternative—in this case, strawberry jam? In many cases, a creative alternative is a good way to defuse perceived problems.

I chose these two attributes, patience and kindness, of this phenomenon we call love as representative of all that is good in our relationship with another person. Remember how the minister or priest spoke of love at your wedding ceremony? They may have used the words from the apostle Paul's letter in the Bible to the young Christians in a city called Corinth. Beginning with verse 4 of chapter 13 we read, "Love is patient, love is kind. It does not envy, it does not boast, it is not proud. It is not rude, it is not self-seeking, it is not easily angered, it keeps no record of wrongs. Love does not delight in evil but rejoices with the truth. It always protects, always trusts, always hopes, always perseveres." The chapter finishes with these familiar words, "And now these three remain: faith, hope and love. But the greatest of these is love" (1 Cor. 13: 4–7, 13).

Love Is Patient, Love Is Kind

Let's just take the first two attributes of love: patience and kindness. Obviously, the rest are also part of making things work within a relationship. I would submit to you that if both parties would practice patience and kindness, we could cut the divorce rate in our country in half. So many things that come our way can make us impatient with each other: an inconvenience that upsets us, something that takes us out of our daily routine or comfort zone, something that makes us late for an appointment or an event, something with the behavior of one of the kids, or maybe a frustration with something or someone at work that makes its way back home—and any little added irritation that sets us off. There are any number of inconveniences or frustrations that bring on an unkind word that are brutal and emotionally hurtful to the one who receives them. Unkind words can spoil everything.

A Flaming Tongue

In the book of James in the New Testament we are warned about the use of the tongue and how cutting it can be: "A bit in the mouth of a horse controls the whole horse. A small rudder on a huge ship in the hands of a skilled captain sets a course in the face of the strongest winds. A word out of your mouth may seem of no account, but it can accomplish nearly anything—or destroy it! It only takes a spark, remember, to set off a forest fire. A careless or wrongly placed word out of your mouth can do that." A verse or two later, James says, "You can tame a tiger, but you can't tame a tongue—it's never been done. . . . With our tongues we bless God our Father; with the same tongues we curse the very men and women he made in his image. Curses and blessings out of the same mouth! My friends, this can't go on" (James 3:3–5, 7–10 MSG). A couple of verses in Proverbs also have a good word for us about the use of our tongue: "A gentle

> Truth be known, if we don't handle our differences in a healthy way, they can become very divisive. "Do not let any unwholesome talk come out of your mouths, but only what is helpful for building up others according to their needs."

answer turns away wrath, but a harsh word stirs up anger" (Prov. 15:1). Also, "The tongue that brings healing is a tree of life, but a deceitful [hurtful] tongue crushes the spirit" (Prov. 15:4).

So when those times come that make us upset, how about taking a deep breath before verbally jabbing at someone? Remember, only a few unkind words can bring distance in your relationship. We would not think of unleashing a verbal barrage on someone outside the family, even a close friend. If we did, it wouldn't be long until that close friend would be a distant friend. So why, then, do we feel we can take it out on someone at home? After all, we say these are the people we love the most. Truth be known, if we don't handle our differences in a healthy way, they can become very divisive. "Do not let any unwholesome talk come out of your mouths, but only what is helpful for building others up according to their needs" (Eph. 4:29).

A little act of patience goes a long way in healing a frustration, or even a disappointment. It can be a way of affirming or encouraging another, when in fact, they thought their error may have caused a big problem. A deep breath, a short walk, or a little time-out for yourself may be a good way to give yourself a few minutes to realize the end of the world is not at hand. Perhaps this proverb says it best: "A patient man has great understanding, but a quick-tempered man displays folly [is a fool]" (Prov. 14:29).

Acts of Kindness

Several years ago, our forty-first president, the late George H. W. Bush, suggested that people practice doing "random acts of kindness." Many thought that was a positive suggestion. So what is kindness? It is going beyond yourself. It is reaching out to help another without expecting anything in return. It is a kind, encouraging word. It may be just a smile and a hello to a stranger that says, "You are important. You count." It is going the extra mile. It is doing something for someone else, even when you may not feel like it, especially within your own home, even when you are dead tired from a full day at work in the jungle out there. Again, it should be regularly practiced within the home. For some reason, it seems easier to reach out to a stranger or friend when help is needed.

A simple illustration of that is the following: A divorcee with two children calls and says her faucet is leaking and she is not sure what to do. You and your wife know her and her kids and would do anything to help her. The husband grabs his tool box and hustles a couple of doors up the street to fix the faucet. Mission accomplished; the faucet has quit leaking. Returning home, the husband feels a sense of helping with a kind act toward a neighbor. The wife commends him for his kindness, but then gently reminds him that they have had a leaky faucet for over three weeks and she has asked him to fix it. Of course, his answer was that he would fix it when he gets a few minutes, which unfortunately never seems to come. However, there is always time to watch the Seattle Seahawks or play a game of golf, and yet in a minute's notice, he has time to fix Mrs. Jones's faucet up the street.

You get my point. Acts of kindness need to be done at home also. There's something to the saying, "Acts of charity must begin at home." The late Barbara Bush, wife of the forty-first president of our country and mother of the forty-third president, reminds us, "Never lose sight of the fact that the most important yardstick of your success will be how you treat other people." That includes the people we say we love the most, our family.

Family Leadership

Patience and kindness are two attributes of a good family leader. All families need good leadership, and a good leader must have the heart of a servant. Good leadership means we lead by example. Jesus reminded us that He "did not come to be served, but to serve" (Mark

10:45). For us men, that means serving our wives and children and even being role models in our service to pets. You can learn a lot about a person's character by how they treat animals.

Leadership does not mean being a dictator, expecting family members to jump on command. It means stepping up and taking charge when needed—marshaling the troops, getting things going, moving things along, making decisions rather than just drifting into letting things happen. My friend Chuck Ferguson, in his book *Indomitable Spirit: Life-Changing Lessons in Leadership*, reminds us that leadership is not always easy, especially when dealing with disappointments and heartaches, having to discipline, and experiencing difficulties and loss. Sometimes leaders have to say and do things that they would choose not to, but they step up and serve for the better good of all involved.[25]

Of course, there needs to be times of discussion with your partner on some decisions, but there are other times when the man just plain needs to step up. I have talked to women who say they have three kids—two children and a husband. They say, "He is so passive and laid back that nothing ever gets done." That can leave her feeling like she needs to take charge, but when asked more than once for help with something, he feels like she is nagging. Not a good situation.

From James Hunter's book, *The Servant*, we read, "The labors of leadership and love are character issues. Patience, kindness, humility, selflessness, respectfulness, forgiveness, honesty, commitment. These character building blocks, or habits, must be developed and matured if we are to become successful leaders who will stand the test of time."[26]

To sum it up, a good leader of his family needs to be seen as a caregiver to his wife and his children. He needs a willingness to serve that manifests itself in a strong quantity of caring with patience and kindness. This is a high calling indeed, but one that binds a family together in caring relationships and provides strong role modeling for his children. Perhaps the apostle Paul's letter to the young Christians in the city of Colossae would be a good summary for this chapter:

> Therefore, as God's chosen people, holy and dearly loved, clothe yourselves with compassion, kindness, humility, gentleness and patience. Bear with each other and forgive whatever grievances you may have against one another. Forgive as the Lord forgave you. And over all these virtues put on love, which binds them together in perfect unity. (Col. 3:12–14)

Going Forward

If you could go shopping in the supermarket of values, what two or three things would you put in your shopping cart and why? What one thing you already have in your cart would you put back on the shelf and why?

Why do you think it is often easier to do things for others outside the family rather than those we live with?

From your perspective, what are the things that prevent people from being kind to others?

What does that word *leadership* mean to you? Can you think of some ways you might be a better leader for your family?

CHAPTER 8

Choosing to Make Changes

Our doubts are traitors, and make us lose the good
we oft might win, by fearing to attempt.
—Shakespeare, *Measure for Measure*

In a *Guideposts* magazine article, I read a story that is so often true it bears repeating. A couple, married for several years, were finding themselves drifting apart. The chase and a lovely wedding had been many, many years before. The husband had been busy in his tech-industry work, later deciding to begin a start-up company. It was taking all his time. His wife had been feeling like she was never a priority. Her emotional loneliness was leaving her hurt and frustrated. Together they decided to take a California coast vacation. Knowing her husband's penchant for work, she was a bit apprehensive that he would not actually keep the commitment. As departure day arrived, she had her bags packed. Sure enough, he decided his work was too important to walk away for a week. The hopes of a relaxing vacation together shattered. As she sought to calm and console her disappointed spirit with prayer, something prodded her to take the vacation anyway. (Call it the "still, small voice" or the "holy nudge.")

He was a bit taken aback that she chose to leave without him, but his company needed him. Not sure if it is the way we men are wired—whether our work can't get along without us or whether it is a lack of caring about our spouse—but somehow we just never quite get on the same page as our mate.

The first few nights, the call home was met with how busy he was. Those were hardly the words, "I miss you." Later that week, as she pulled into another hotel, she was met with a big surprise: her husband was there. As they talked, he recounted how he had missed her, how he decided he would give up his start-up company, and how he was going back to his former job at the high-tech company. He had decided things had to change.[27] Hello!

Change Is Not Easy

Why does it take so long for the light to go on for men? Doing something different, out of our routine, is hard to come by for many of us. Change does not come easy. Most of us like a standard routine, whether it be work times, meal times, or going-to-bed times. Our body gets into a routine. Making a change can be anything from an inconvenience to just plain disruptive. The hard part is that it leaves us feeling out of control. Routine has us in control. Routine can also make us predictable, complacent, and frankly, sometimes boring.

As time moves along in our daily routines, the excitement and joy of

> As time moves along in our daily routines, the excitement and joy of living subsides, and we lapse into the unemotional daily phase of just grinding it out. Is this something we want to continue?

living subsides, and we lapse into the unemotional daily phase of just grinding it out. Is this something we want to continue? We have a way of just muddling through life if we don't occasionally throw in some variety like a long weekend away, a week's vacation, or even a monthly date night.

As I stated earlier, men especially have a difficult time moving out of the comfort zone. This is especially true when problems arise in a marriage, when the husband and wife begin to look at their mate's faults rather than seeing each other as a valued person and focusing on how they can meet each other's needs.

Problems—Whose Fault?

Unfortunately, men often look at these marriage difficulties as the woman's problem. From the Olsen personal file here: I would often visit my father at a local convalescent center during the last few months he was there. One day as we chatted, I brought up an apparent unpleasant subject: his and Mom's yearlong separation. My question was, "Dad, now that I do family counseling, I am wondering what you saw as the reason for you and Mom splitting for that year?"

Dad's response; "I never could figure out what your mother's problem was." Of course, he saw it as her problem, and of course, he had nothing to do with it. If she would have just gotten her act together, everything would have been fine. That is how he and many men see any issue in the marriage.

Now, personal input from me: something about "the acorn doesn't fall far from the oak tree." When things seemed to be going sour between my former wife and me, I had no idea how to respond. I felt I was a good husband. I tried to be a good father to our children. I felt like I took care of things around the home: yard work, automobiles, etc. I was faithful in my job and helped with the children and their activities. Yet unfortunately, I was far too involved with my work.

I was missing the interaction and dialogue with my wife, and ultimately, I caused her emotional pain as the distance between us grew. Like most men, I felt like we could work through it. I became more frustrated and began to clam up, more staying the course than willing to take a good look at what was really happening. She suggested counseling, but I felt we could work through it. Unfortunately, good intentions didn't get it done.

I look back now and see where I was unwilling to make some changes to attempt to get the relationship back on track. As I have alluded to earlier, there is something about the way men are wired that makes us think we can be in control and things will work out. Rather, if we would be a willing participant to our wife's intuitions, we would do far better in keeping the relationship alive. Take it from one who has been there; when your wife says, "Honey, we need to talk," be willing to sit down and *listen attentively* rather than thinking a tweak in your work schedule, a vase of flowers, or a quick fix on the washer or dryer (or whatever appliance needs work) will cure the problem. It probably goes much deeper than that. Most likely it requires dealing with the emotional side of the relationship. Maybe it even means addressing some abuse factor that you are not even aware of, or the hurt you are causing.

In summary, I would say Shakespeare had it right as I quoted earlier: "Our doubts are traitors, and make us lose the good we oft might win, by fearing to attempt." Men, when your mate is feeling a need for some changes, see this as a positive. Work with her on what changes seem appropriate, and implement a new dimension that will lead to new horizons within the relationship. Your willingness to flex could be a significant move toward that once-appreciated courtship nurturing pattern.

Going Forward

Coffee cup time again.

Hindsight is always twenty-twenty. If you could change one or two things in your earlier relationship with your spouse, what would they be?

If life is a process and subject to changes, what rough edges could change at this stage in your relationship? What is holding you back from those changes?

CHAPTER 9

A Message for Men

As iron sharpens iron, so one man sharpens another.
—Proverbs 27:17

Throughout history, many men and women have had mentors to help guide them, especially through difficult times. Many a role model has guided a young person toward a correct path, be it a Boy or Girl Scout leader, a youth pastor, a Young Life leader, a coach, a neighbor friend, or some other significant adult. Many adults can look back to a person who was a role model or a mentor who guided them through the uncertainties of the teen years while opinions and mindsets were forming and impacting their lives.

Eventually, as one moves to adulthood, the natural instinct is a moving toward the chase. In most cases, the male acts on instinct, and what he deems to be the right thing in his mind may or may not be so, often depending on what transpired in his home life as he grew up. Even if his mother and father had a good marriage, he is now on his own.

He may have read a book or two on marriage prior to the big day (most likely not), and that may have been his preparation for married life. Maybe he even had some counseling sessions. Compare this illustration to learning to swim. You can read books on swimming, but until you venture into the pool or lake, you won't learn how to swim. So also in marriage. You are starting from scratch in a lifelong learning process. Having a mentor will prove to be a big factor in your success as a soul mate to your spouse. I will elaborate more on this later in the chapter.

As I stated in my introduction, hopefully you men have picked up on the concept of this book: encouragement to make your marriage all that you wanted it to be when you said, "I do." With this in mind, I have included a chapter specifically for you. Your partner may want to read this and may have other suggestions. I have provided significant suggestions I hope you will take seriously. If you are willing to do so, I honestly believe you will fan some burning embers and bring more flame and warmth into your relationship. For some of you, the flame is well lit, but you feel you just need a booster shot. Hopefully this will give you that added push.

For others of you, the embers are barely smoldering, nearly on their last gasp of oxygen. They may be, in your mind, beyond reigniting. Remember what I said in an earlier chapter: "The present situation is not the final destination"—unless you want it to be, of course. To you I would say, "Give hope a chance." I should mention that some of those things I suggest will mean making changes. As I said in the last chapter, change is never easy. In fact, for some, choosing to make changes may be downright difficult, maybe even painful, because it takes us out of the routine and our comfort zone. It may prove to be downright inconvenient to the point of frustration. Hang in there; better things are to come, though it will take time. Let me give you some suggestions for getting back on track.

Back to Square One—Praise, Please, and Thank You

How about beginning with what you did in those earlier days—a phone call during the day to let the other person know you are thinking of them? Men, how about opening the car door for your mate—a nice courtesy? How about holding hands when walking together? How about holding the chair as she is being seated at the dinner table? You probably did these things when the courtship was in full bloom. Why did you stop? Is she less valued? These little things can be very meaningful to both of you.

Here is something very simple. We'll call it baby steps. How about "please" and "thank you"? I know you may think it elementary or stupid, but those little words can make a huge difference. My wife and I try to include them in our everyday conversation. "Thank you for fixing dinner tonight." (By the way, Mardi usually fixes dinner, and I do the dishes, including pots and pans. We like to talk like we are a team.) "I like your new haircut, Mardi." "You really look nice today." "That's a nice-looking outfit."

Women like to be complimented on their appearance. Did you catch that sentence? It is so important, I am going to repeat it: *Women like to be complimented on their appearance!* "I appreciate you doing the wash today so I can have clean clothes." "Those new flowers you planted in our garden look great." "I appreciate you changing those messy diapers all day." Or let her know you would like to take the kids for the weekend so she could have some time away with her girlfriends, or even a girl's night out. You'll discover that taking care of the kids day in and day out is a real job. You won't be coming home after your workday and ask, "What did you do all day?"

Teamwork Pays Off

In today's society, we have a new normal when it comes to family teamwork. In my growing years, fathers brought home the paycheck and contributed biologically so kids could enter the family. Mothers took care of the home front, along with looking after the kids' needs, cooking, cleaning, doing laundry, and sometimes working in the yard. Today's new normal has mothers working full- or part-time jobs, as well as doing all the work the home front demands. That is why it is imperative that fathers pitch in and help with much more of the home and kid responsibilities.

My dad saw his responsibility as just bringing home the paycheck. My mother also worked full-time and seemingly took care of everything at home with help from us boys as we got older. I don't mean to put my father down. He did what most men thought was right, providing monetarily for the family, which was what their role models had taught them. Everything else was left to the woman. Things have changed today with many women working full-time and more men pitching in to help around the home, as it should be.

You can see my drift on this subject. It becomes a matter of teamwork, encouragement, and building the other person up. It is no secret; simple helps, along with affirmation and encouragement, say, "I love you" in a special way, and often they are reciprocated. Men also need to hear affirmation and encouragement because that is a big part of them feeling respected. Let me repeat that for you women: *Men also need to hear affirmation and encouragement because that is a big part of them feeling respected.* "Thank you for getting up early and going to work today so we

> Men also need to hear affirmation and encouragement because that is a big part of them feeling respected.

could have food on the table." "Thank you for fixing the car today so I don't have to worry about it." "Thank you for cleaning the garage." "The yard looks really good; I appreciate your cutting and edging the lawn." "The garden looks great; thank you for weeding it." "That shirt and tie make a good outfit for you."

Remember what I shared earlier: "Happiness is like a perfume. You cannot give to others without getting a few drops on yourself." In summary: Men, you are in control on this affirmation/encouragement suggestion. You can choose to do this or not. Women seem to be wired to understand the ins and outs of this encouragement thing. For men, it must be a conscious choice.

Balancing Family and Work

Most men have jobs that are demanding, some with over-demanding pressure.. That is the trick as far as a relationship goes—balancing work and family. It is not an easy task, especially when you know the high demands at work. Referring back to chapter 8, this was the case of a couple I wrote about where work had taken over the husband's life. Eventually, he realized what was really important and put some priorities in place.

A doctor I know was curious regarding my earlier book about fathers and the role they play in raising emotionally healthy children. I said I was committed to helping fathers understand how very much their children needed them, especially during the elementary school years. He told me that his wife and kids were important to him and he gives them a lot of time. He then said that if his medical practice ever took precedence over his time with his family, he would leave the medical field. He is a smart man who has his priorities figured out and won't be overrun by his workload. My guess is that he smartly prioritizes his life in terms of relationships in the following order: God, family, friends, and work. That's not to say that work isn't important, but he refuses to let it override those things that are most important. As Dick and Ruth Foth state in their book on friendship, *KNOWN*, "Life revolves around two things—relationships and money. And only one of those makes us rich. . . . We are not talking properties or portfolios."[28]

Actually, many men are aware of the kids' games or other activities missed, the wife's disappointment at missing a special date you and she had planned, and the times a greatly anticipated event had to be postponed, all in the name of "my work." I don't deny that there are times when something at work interrupts plans. A wife understands that can happen, especially if it is a rare occasion and if the work/family balancing act has the right priorities. Again, this is where the balancing comes in. Maybe the two of you need to sit down with your calendars and devise a schedule with *some things you both can look forward to.* Maybe it is a special night out—at least a once-a-month dinner, movie, concert, ice cream sundae night, etc. Having something to look forward to is always special. Anticipation of something special, something to look forward to days or weeks out, can be a spirit lifter. Or maybe once or twice a month the family has a talk-it-over time for an hour or two over some ice cream, discussing things like highlights, lowlights, upcoming events, family vacation plans, home improvements, etc., without the interruption of TV or cell phones. Whatever works for you, set your schedule in ink on the calendar and realize the importance of following through.

Presents Are Good; Your Presence Is Better

Men, be willing to lighten up on the work schedule so your wife does not feel you are married to your work and that she is your mistress when you have the time. Note: sometimes men hope to replace the void at home with gifts. Men, your wife and kids need your presence, not presents. They most of all want you, not gifts. As wonderful as gifts can be, the best gift for them is you. They need to know they are truly valued, and your time with them assures them they are high on your list of priorities. Today, families are so active that it is hard to even think about setting a time just to sit down and talk.

Variety Eases the Routine

One of the comments I often hear is, "My husband is so predictable. He's boring." Again, it's about *balancing family and the routine of work.*

Most people like to have some variety in life, even some adventure that takes you out of your comfort zone. I'm not necessarily talking about bungee jumping or skydiving, but something different from the daily routine. Perhaps it means a day hike to a mountain lake, a bicycle ride for lunch somewhere, taking the kids to the zoo, a ferry boat ride, a day at a local fair, or maybe a longer trip and an overnight stay at some lodge. It may be something that doesn't cost an arm and a leg or something the two of you have had on your bucket list and have made plans and saved for. It means that anything that takes you out of the daily humdrum routine is always welcome and adds something extra to the relationship. I might add here that when you do something out of the ordinary, *stay away from your cell phone*. I know this will be difficult, but remember, this is family time. You scheduled it. Focus on your wife and children. If you are on your phone, you might as well be at the office. Accept no calls. Turn it off. Use it only for emergencies.

A Mentor Is a Must

It is good to have someone you can regard as a close friend, as the Scripture says, one "who sticks closer than a brother" (Prov. 18:24). This should be a person you can confide in both in the good times and in the troubling, stressful times, someone you can count on to hang in there with you through those difficult situations, someone who will pray for you for wisdom and guidance in the midst of uncertainty and help you see a positive outcome clearly. Truly, iron does sharpen iron, and one man sharpens another (Prov. 27:17).

Whether it is a single individual or a small group of men, I cannot emphasize enough the importance of investing some of your time in the presence of a mentor, or in the case of a small group, a few mentors.

Let me give you an example of each. As a high school senior, I became a Christian through the Young Life program with some friends at my high school. Entering university, I had begun going to church, but I really wasn't growing in my journey as a young Christian. I knew I should read the Bible, but I didn't seem to be picking up much. I was in touch with a fellow who was a year older than me and who was a Christian. I simply asked him if he would be willing to help me grow in my faith. He was more than willing. Each Thursday afternoon I would meet him on the University of Washington campus in Seattle, and we would drive to the UW arboretum, which has several acres of beautiful trees, shrubs, and flowers not far from campus. We would talk about how things were going in general, and then read from the Bible and pray together, confining it to just one hour because we were both quite busy. He would explain various aspects of the Bible and answer my questions about theology. Couple that with attending worship services on Sunday and the college-age group on Tuesday evenings, and I began to build a foundation in my faith. Roots were taking hold. Looking back, it was so significant to have a mentor who helped me develop my early faith. Over the years and even today, I have had the opportunity to pay it forward and mentor others. One-on-one communication can be so significant in the mentoring process. It is a good example of iron sharpening iron.

The Value of a Small Group

Other help in growing as a Christian can come from what is called a covenant group—just a small group of guys who get together on a regular basis, usually weekly, who may have a meal together, read from Scripture (usually a passage or a chapter), discuss, and pray for any needs and concerns that need attention. One such group I participated in was with close friends who met for many years. Today we are separated by cross-country distances, but we still stay in touch, concerned about each other's families and activities.

The essence of these covenant groups involves several characteristics and principles. I list a few of them here, having drawn some information from a chapter in my previous book on fatherhood.[29]

1. The Covenant of Affirmation: There is nothing you have done or will do to make me stop loving you. I will love you as a person and do all I can to hold you up in God's affirming love.

2. The Covenant of Confidentiality: I promise to keep whatever is shared within the group confidential in order to allow each member to feel safe enough to share.

3. The Covenant of Prayer: I promise to pray for your needs on a regular basis.

4. The Covenant of Availability: Anything I have—time, energy, insight, possessions—are at your disposal if you should need them. If you need me, I am here for you.

5. The Covenant of Honesty: I promise to be honest, a man of integrity. I promise to speak the truth in love.

6. The Covenant of Accountability: I promise to ask for your help in being accountable to God and to you for becoming more fully who God designed me to be.

Accountability Is Significant

A key ingredient of a covenant group is accountability. Everyone needs to be accountable to someone, and we should ask that "someone" to encourage us in the areas of honesty, integrity, ethics, and the values that keep us on the higher road. *Accountability* is not a bad word. It is simply choosing to hold yourself responsible to stay on the high road as you journey on in life. Unfortunately, men often feel they need

> *Accountability* is not a bad word. It is simply choosing to hold yourself to the high road.

to be strong in character, unemotional, successful, a good person. They have been schooled to never show their feelings, failures, warts, or any weaknesses. Not wanting to show any vulnerability, they wear a mask of respectability. The truth is, bridges of friendship are built when we can safely reveal our fears, failings, and difficulties.

Another illustration of why accountability is so important is in our journey: remember the illustration in chapter 6 about testing rockets in the space program? If off course shortly after launch, the rocket would be destroyed because far down the missile range it would be way off course. So it is with our lives. A little sin can easily become a big sin and eventually have us way off course, whether it be stealing, cheating, or an affair. It may start small, but it can become full-blown in a hurry. Therefore, see accountability as one of the most important, positive aspects of your life. Desire it to keep you at your best. As the writer of Proverbs admonishes us, "Keep your heart with all vigilance, for from it flow the springs of life" (Prov. 4:23 RSV).

An Addiction That Destroys You

What I am going to share with you next is life-threatening. It is another illustration that will show you what happens when you are not accountable. Let us take a look at the fastest growing addiction. Researchers now say that 25 percent of internet search engine requests are for pornography.[30] What begins as a simple watching of some scantily clad woman or titillating nude pictures can easily lead to an obsession. Since we men operate so much on the visual, it is not hard to see why we can get dragged into pornography rather easily.

Our news reports are full of stories where someone is picked up for pornography, often child porn. Whether a person is arrested or not, pornography has a horrible effect on the brain for those who get sucked into this addiction. Don't think, *This would never happen to me.* One source I read says, "Pornography watching can become a compulsive practice, and once those pleasure connections are created in the brain, they can be very difficult to break. It can ruin your life."[31] Our brains are wired with billions of special nerves (neurons) that carry electrical signals back and forth between parts of the brain and send out signals to the rest of our body.[32] Repeated consumption of pornography causes the brain to rewire itself. It triggers the brain to pump out chemicals and form new pathways, leading to profound, and not so good, lasting changes in the brain.[33] Though some effort has been made to disprove the connection between the brain and pornography, there is enough evidence to show a correlation. For more study on the adverse effects of pornography, look up "How Porn Changes the Brain—Fight the New Drug" on the internet.

A good summary of the effects of pornography comes from Dr. Gregory Jantz in his book, *Battles Men Face*. He states:

> Pornography promises to make you feel like more of a man and then works to strip away the values of manhood. It wrests control of your choices and decisions from you, rendering you impotent against it; it perverts how you view and appreciate women, corrupting your most intimate relationships; it exchanges the deeper satisfaction of living an honorable life for cheap, temporary thrills; it erodes your natural compassion and desire to protect women and instead exploits them for personal satisfaction. Pornography warps who you are as a man. As such, pornography is your enemy, one out to destroy you.[34]

Unfortunately, just like drug addiction, pornography addiction takes a toll on many people. An acquaintance of mine was into pornography. He is now in federal prison. He certainly didn't plan it that way, but eventually the addiction helped to push him into further inappropriate behavior. Addiction has a way of doing that. He would probably deny that he has an addiction, that he made a bad choice, or that a government sting brought him down. Honestly, we can choose to do what we want in life, but we cannot choose the consequences. From my perspective, he chose not to be accountable to anyone who could help him to stay on the "narrow road that leads to life." Unfortunately, he chose the broad road that "leads to destruction" as described in Matthew 7:13–14. Choose early on to make a definite commitment not to look at pornography. It is a choice you have to make.

Having a mentor, realizing the accountability factor (whether it be with an individual or in a small covenant group), and smart choices will help keep you on the high road that leads to life. Men, I hope the suggestions of this chapter will be of help to you. Remember, "As iron sharpens iron, so one man sharpens another." I implore you—be accountable to someone!

Going Forward

On a scale of one to ten (ten being well-balanced), how would you rate your balance of family and work? Why? Does your spouse agree with you? Why or why not?

In what ways do you see a mentor being of help?

Why do you see accountability as valuable?

After reading this chapter, what do you feel you need to do differently and why? What will keep you from following through with your good intentions?

CHAPTER 10

Faith and Love Going Forward

Take time for quiet moments, as God whispers and the world is very loud.
—Author Unknown

In the late fourth and early fifth centuries, a noted North African theologian and philosopher had a profound influence on what was to become Western Christianity with his writing and perspective on the nature of God. He is often referred to as the Doctor of the Church and is revered as one of the most important church fathers in all of Western Christianity. He is recognized as a saint in the Catholic Church, the Eastern Christian Church, and the Anglican community. We know him as St. Augustine of Hippo, (the region of Regius in North Africa).

One of St. Augustine's most profound thoughts is the following: "Thou has made us for thyself, O Lord, and our heart is restless until it finds its rest in thee."[35] In this statement, St. Augustine is attesting to the fact that the God who breathed the breath of life into each of us wants to take His rightful place in our hearts. Until that happens, we will sense a restless spirit and often find ourselves thinking about life with the words, "What's it all about?" It may not be an overwhelming feeling of "What's going on?" but in the subconscious we sense that things aren't quite right. In the great scheme of world events it may not seem very important, but in each individual life it is very significant, being rightly related to the God who formed you and gave you life.

It's All about Relationships

Over the years, I have concluded that life is all about relationships—being rightly related to God and to those around us, including our spouse, our children, our extended family and friends, and our fellow workers. When any of those are out of whack, our inner spirit feels it. No doubt, there is a need to make things right, and I have covered that in the chapter on forgiveness. In this chapter I will focus on two primary relationships: our relationship with God and our relationship with our partner.

In Genesis we read, "In the beginning God created the heavens and the earth" (Gen. 1:1). Those beautiful snow-covered mountains, gigantic oceans, beasts of the field, birds of the air, and fish of the sea just didn't show up one day and fall into place. Simply put, there is a Creator—God. I hope you see this as a given. Likewise, we, too, are part of His handiwork: "So God created man in his own image, in the image of God he created him; male and female he created them" (Gen. 1:27). The psalmist records a good reminder of our God's creative ability. I recorded this in an earlier chapter, but it is so important for our understanding, I am repeating it:

> For you created my inmost being; you knit me together in my mother's womb. I praise you because I am fearfully made; your works are wonderful, I know that full well. My

frame was not hidden from you when I was made in the secret place. When I was woven together in the depths of the earth, your eyes saw my unformed body. All the days ordained for me were written in your book before one of them came to be. (Ps. 139:13–16)

Thus, it stands to reason that God, who created life, would also give His creation some sort of instruction on how to live as He would want us to live. The psalmist records, "Teach us to number our days aright, that we may gain a heart of wisdom" (Ps. 90:12). In essence, in our days here on this earth, we are to desire to know God's ways and be wise in following them. Wisdom can be defined in many ways. A wise person can be one who makes good judgments, one who is prudent, one who has keen insight, one who uses common sense, or one who gains knowledge. I should mention here that knowledge and wisdom don't necessarily mean the same thing. A humorous illustration shows you what I mean: Knowledge says a tomato is a fruit. Wisdom says you don't put a tomato in a fruit salad.

A Heart of Wisdom

Gaining a heart of wisdom from a biblical perspective means we see things from God's point of view as we seek to consistently follow His instruction. Contrast this to how we would typically respond in different situations.

- The natural way to respond when someone wrongs us is to get back at them, or as we might say, "to get even." Jesus says when someone wrongs you, you forgive them, just as the Lord has forgiven you (Matt. 6:14–15.)
- The natural way for people is to just get by—do what is expected and not much more. Jesus implores us to do more

than just what is expected of us. He says to go the extra mile (Matt. 5:41.)

- The natural desire for some people is to have others serve them in one way or another. Jesus reminds us of a better way by His words and by His example. Jesus did not come to be served, but to serve. One's goodness and greatness is found in serving (Matt. 20:26–28.)

- The natural way is to love those who love you and forget those who don't seem to care about you. It is so easy to judge people and write off the ones you don't like. Jesus says that we are to love every person, even those who would persecute us or be judgmental of us (Matt. 5:43–48; 7:1–5.)

- Many people exalt themselves and their position in life. Jesus says to humble yourself. In doing so, you will be exalted (Matt. 23:12.)

As you can see, gaining a heart of wisdom takes on a whole new meaning when we see things from our Lord's point of view and from His instruction. Amazing! What a difference it makes in a relationship when life is lived the way our Creator intended us to live. *A person of wisdom will gladly accept instruction.*

The truth is, we choose to live and to do the things we want. God will not force us. He has given us free choice. Yes, we can choose to do the things we want; however, we cannot choose the consequences. Again,

> God's plan for your life far exceeds the circumstances of your day.

here is a simple illustration: if you choose to speed in your car, the consequence could be a citation. Our mandate, then, is to choose to follow our Creator's instruction as related to us in the Bible, His playbook, our manual for living. "God's plan for your life far exceeds the circumstances of your day."[36]

No One Is Perfect

God's instruction also helps us get back on track when we have erred. As I stated earlier, not one of us is perfect. We all have our warts and fall short in word and deed. The Bible refers to our error as sin, which is not a popular word because it infers a shortcoming on our part, and none of us likes to think we fall short. To show you how offensive the word *sin* is, if I walked into a room and said, "You're all sinners," everyone would be deeply insulted and probably yell back at me. That word grates on us. If I walked into that same room and said, "We all make mistakes" or "Nobody's perfect" or "We all fall short of what we should be and do," there would probably be a nodding of heads in agreement. Most likely no one would be upset. Sin means we are out of the relationship with God. That estrangement from God means separation now and in the life to come. That is the penalty for our sinfulness.

To rectify the situation in marriage where distance and estrangement are present, there must be some sort of communication and forgiveness if there is to be newness of life and a marriage that finds its way back on track. Likewise with God. The good news is that God has provided a way for us to once again be in a relationship with Him even if we have unintentionally, or intentionally, come off the rails.

Our God has loved us enough and wants to have a relationship with us, so much so that He has provided a way. The Bible says, "The law requires that nearly everything be cleansed with blood, and without the shedding of blood there is no forgiveness" (Heb. 9:22).

Most of us realize that blood is a cleaning agent. If you get a snakebite or bug bite, you try to squeeze out some blood to bring the venom out with it. So it is that Jesus shed His blood as He died on the cross to pay the penalty for our sins. (We celebrate this on Good Friday and His resurrection on Easter.) When we decide that our priority is a relationship with the God who gave us life, we are choosing to begin a lifelong journey with the Lord Jesus. The first step is to invite Him into our lives with a simple prayer like the one below. In sincerely reciting this prayer or something similar, you are inviting Jesus Christ into your life.

> *Lord Jesus*, please come into my life and be my Savior and Lord. Please forgive my sins and give me the gift of eternal life.

Be assured that if you prayed that prayer or something similar, our Lord heard you, for He stated in the book of Revelation, "I stand at the door [of your heart] and knock. If anyone hears my voice and opens the door, I will come in and eat [fellowship] with him, and he with me" (Rev. 3:20).

A New Beginning

The Bible also says, "Therefore, if anyone is in Christ, he is a new creation; the old has gone, the new has come!" (2 Cor. 5:17). Or as another translation has put it, "The old has passed away, behold, the new has come.

" (2 Cor. 5:17 RSV). So, in a very real sense, you have been born again and are beginning a new spiritual journey.

Of course, once you take this step, you will need some help in growing in your Christian life. Like a newborn baby entering the world, it is important in those early days to receive some help on your journey. Perhaps you have a Christian friend or a pastor. Remember, in a previous chapter I mentioned it would be good to have a mentor to help you grow spiritually. If your spouse is a Christian, he or she may help you get started or refer you to someone. This is not a time to hold back. Desire some help. Find someone who can give you guidance as you begin your spiritual journey. Spiritual growth will not just happen any more than a newborn could survive without help.

A New Perspective

Now I want to give you a tip to enrich your relationship with your partner. Remember the chart in chapter 6 that told about the communication patterns that couples build? At the very top of the triangle was God, who designed marriage. You both said your "I dos" in a covenant with God and headed for the reception and the honeymoon. Let's go back to the triangle I designed for you.

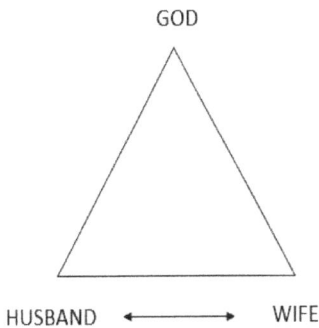

GOD

HUSBAND ←———→ WIFE

Figure 1

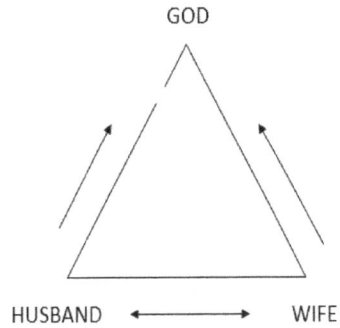

GOD

HUSBAND ←———→ WIFE

Figure 2

You will notice that on the bottom corners of the triangles I have put *husband* and *wife*. In most problem-solving situations, husband and wife go back and forth, trying to come to some sort of amicable solution (Fig. 1). Sometimes arguing or blaming takes over. The back-and-forth is represented by the arrow going both ways in the give-and-take of discussions. You will notice that in this scenario the husband and wife remain at the corners and do not seem to draw closer to each other.

Let us look at another scenario. If the husband and wife focus on God in their daily lives, then look to the Lord and His teaching and follow His ways, as represented by the upward flow of the arrows, they will grow closer together, just as the lines get closer together as they move upward (Fig. 2). As they seek to follow Jesus of Nazareth and His ways, their lives take on new meaning, direction, and purpose within themselves and for each other. That doesn't mean they won't have differences and some struggles, but there can be a greater understanding as they seek to come to agreements. This is letting love go forward with God's help. The prophet Jeremiah has some good words for us: "'For I know the plans I have for you,' declares the Lord, 'plans to prosper you and not to harm you, plans to give you hope and a future'" (Jer. 29:11).

A New Look at the Prodigal

To better explain the depth of God's love, I share a familiar story. Many already know the outcome, but for some, it may be the first time you have heard it. If you have never considered a relationship with God, please heed these words. In fact, this may prove to be the most significant chapter in this book. If you follow through with this information, you will have discovered a vital secret of life.

This is the story of the Prodigal Son (Luke 15:11–24). He is the fellow who got tired of working on his father's property and decided he wanted a different lifestyle. His father gave him his inheritance, and he went off to live a life of extravagance. In time, the money ran out and he desired to come home.

Let's re-imagine this biblical parable in modern times. (A parable is a fictitious narrative that embodies a spiritual truth.) Suppose a young man was working in an apple orchard on the family farm in the Yakima Valley of Washington State. It was not an easy life: hot sun, long hours, the toils of farm life with animals and crops, grinding it out each day. One day the young man decided he has had enough and wants to set out on his own for something different than what he has known on the farm. He talked his father into giving him what would be his inheritance, and he headed for the bright lights of the Bay Area in California. There he lived it up with a lifestyle far different from his life on the farm, eventually using up all his money on his new pleasures.

While wondering about life and where he would go next for lodging and a meal, *he came to his senses.* He had a sudden change of heart, realizing all he had given up for a few months of pleasure. He surmised that even the animals and the hired men on the farm back home were doing better than he was at the moment. He decided to go home if his father would take him back. With only a few dollars left, he called home and talked to a family member who said his father was out working in the field. The family member wasn't so sure his father would want him back. The son told the person on the other end of the line to ask his father to put a yellow ribbon on one of the trees in the orchard near the train tracks if he wanted him back. Because the train he would be riding on passed by the orchard, the young man would see the yellow ribbon and know that the father wanted him home. With his last dollars, the young man purchased a train ticket home.

The orchard was up the tracks a long way from where the son would get off at the train depot. As the train neared the orchard, the young man became overly anxious. What if there was no yellow ribbon? As the anxiety and the possibility of rejection set in, he asked the conductor to look out the window as they approached the orchard and to let him know if he saw a yellow ribbon on any branch of any tree in the orchard. The young man, being so uneasy, looked the other way.

After passing the orchard, the young man rather hesitantly asked the conductor, "Did you see a yellow ribbon on any tree in the orchard?"

With a caring, warm smile on his face, the conductor said, "Son, I saw a yellow ribbon on every branch of every tree in your father's orchard."

Do you think that father wanted his son home? Of course he did. To finish the analogy of the parable, God wants us all to come home to Him. He has provided a way, through the payment of the penalty for our sinfulness of wandering off to do what we thought was going to make life good. The Prodigal Son thought the ways of the world would fit him well, just as all of us have seen fit to err in one way or another.

Our heavenly Father, in His great mercy, sent His son to give us a better life by dying on the cross to pay the penalty for our sin and for the times we have run from Him. His forgiveness of our sin is complete in the death and resurrection of His Son.

In a very real sense, there is a yellow ribbon on every branch of every tree saying to each of us, "Come home." A loving heavenly Father says, "I love you," as expressed in His Son, Jesus Christ. If you have never considered this before, the Lord is waiting for you at the train station. He wants to welcome you with open arms, and as you step off that train, He would give you a caring hug and gently whisper, "I love you. I am so glad you have come home. There is a place at the table, set for you. I want to walk with you on the rest of your journey on this earth."

A Time to Recalculate

Here is a final thought as we finish this book. One electronic device of great help to drivers is the GPS direction guide. Mardi and I use it all the time when taking a road trip or anytime in town when we are unsure of a new destination or when heavy traffic dictates a different route. You simply put in your starting point or current location and add your destination. As you travel, you are reminded what turns to take, how many miles before the next turn, how

> If you have never considered this before, the Lord is waiting for you at the train station. He wants to welcome you with open arms, and as you step off that train, He would give you a hug and gently whisper, "I love you. I am so glad you have come home."

long it will take to reach your destination, etc. It is a marvelous tool to assist drivers. Every now and then when we decide to take a different route or divert from the original instruction, we hear a voice (we call her Hazel) say, "Recalculating." Obviously, we have thrown Hazel a curve and she must recalculate her directions to us. "She" is aware we have changed course and is resetting the instructions.

As we move along life's road, sometimes we all need to take time to recalculate. Maybe it is a small alteration; maybe it is a big-time adjustment. This is especially true when your heart and mind have taken in new information that could make you the person you want to be and the person your partner needs you to be.

Perhaps this is one of those times in your life, knowing how much God loves you and how much you love your family. It's time for some quiet moments to recalculate and make some adjustments. It is my hope that this book has been a wake-up call and has prompted the still, small voice to say, "Time for some changes."

Let Love Go Forward

. . . from this time and place

Going Forward

Time to have a wrap-up chat on the book. By the way, these coffee cup chats should just be the start of joining with your partner often for times of discussion.

Thinking through the reading of this book, the things I learned are:

In recalculating, I make the promise that I will do the following:

Endnotes

Chapter 1

1 Statistics are taken from the U.S. Census Bureau, as recorded in Wikipedia. https://en.wikipedia.org/wiki/United_States_Census_Bureau

Chapter 2

2 CNN—Travel, Emanuella Granberg, June 1, 2015.

3 "10 Awesome Love Locks Locations Around the World," 10MostToday.com, June 11, 2014, https://10mosttoday.com/10-awesome-love-locks-locations-from-around-the-world/.

4 Paraphrased from the song title by Nina Simone, "You've got to Learn."

5 Mark Pearson, words from his song "Let Love Go Forward." Used by permission.

Chapter 3

6 Family Insights was a nonprofit corporation in which I held seminars, workshops, retreats, etc., primarily to men on their significant role in raising emotionally healthy children. As I aged and had some health issues, I chose to close the Family Insights Corp., and the domain name was secured by someone else.

7 Terry Olsen, *My Father, My Hero: Becoming Your Child's Best Friend* (Enumclaw, WA: WinePress Publishing, 1995).

8 Quote attributed to Zig Ziglar. https://goodreads.com/quotes/915549

9 Helen Colton, *The Gift of Touch: How Physical Contact Improves Communication, Pleasure, and Health* (New York: Putnam Publishing Group, 1983).

10 Virginia Satir (1916–1988), from her biography, Good Therapy.org, https://www.goodtherapy.org/famous-psychologists/virginia-satir.html.

11 Dr. Gary Chapman, *The 5 Love Languages* (Chicago: Northfield Publishing 1992), 107.

12 Quote attributed to several people including Mahatma Gandhi, Stephen Grellet, Quaker William Penn, and Ralph Waldo Emerson.

Chapter 4

13 Edgar Guest poem, "A Friend's Greeting." https://www.best-poems.net/edgar-guest/friends-greeting.html

14 Author unknown. Hallmark greeting card.

15 A. A. Milne, *Winnie the Pooh* (New York: Dutton Children's Books, 1926). Also, https://goodreads.com/author/quote/81466A_A_Milne?page=2.

Chapter 5

16 Erma Bombeck, *If Life Is A Bowl Of Cherries, Why Am I Always In The Pits.* New York Ballantine Books, Division of Random House

17 Charles Swindoll, https://quoteland.com/author/Charles-Swindoll-Quote/1301/.

18 The original collection of these sayings was created by a college student named Kent M. Keith and was published by Harvard Student Agencies in 1968 in a pamphlet entitled, "The Silent Revolution: Dynamic Leadership in the Student Council."

19 Bruce Larson, *There's a Lot More to Health Than Not Being Sick* (Waco: Word Books, 1971), 28.

Chapter 6

20 Statistics from the National Center For Health Statistics, https://www.avvo.com/legal-guides/ugc..marriage-divorce-statistics.

21 Olsen, *My Father, My Hero.* The chart from this chapter of Let Love Go Forward is found on page 63 of My Father, My Hero.

22 Dr. Gregory L. Jantz, *Healing the Scars of Emotional Abuse* (Grand Rapids: Fleming H. Revell, 1995), 27.

23 A variation of this saying has been attributed to Maya Angelou, Carl Buehner, and others. Carl Buehner is believed to have been the first to have used it.

24 Charlie W. Shedd, *Letters to Philip* (Old Tappan, NJ: Fleming H. Revell Co., 1973), 84.

Chapter 7

25 Chuck Ferguson and Steve Duin, *Indomitable Spirit: Life-Changing Lessons in Leadership* (Portland, OR: Agora Publishing, 2013), 73.

26 James C. Hunter, *The Servant* (New York: Crown Publishing Group, 1998), 167.

Chapter 8

27 Andrea Owan, "Road Trip," *Guideposts*, May 2017, 64–67.

Chapter 9

28 Dick Foth and Ruth Foth, *KNOWN* New York: Waterbrook, 2017), 16.

29 Olsen, *My Father, My Hero,* 178–179.

30 Collective Evolution, "The Science of Pornography Addiction and What It Can Do to Your Brain," https://www.collective-evolution.com/2016/03/07/the-science-of-pornography-addiction-what-it-can-do-to-your-brain/.

31 Ibid.

32 Dr. Norman Doidge, *The Brain That Changes Itself* (New York: Penguin Books, 2007).

33 https://fightthenewdrug.org/how-porn-changes-the-brain/

34 Dr. Gregory L. Jantz, *Battles Men Face* (Grand Rapids: Fleming H. Revell 2012), 30.

Chapter 10

35 Wikipeida Encyclopedia, "St. Augustine, Nov. 354 - Aug.430."

36 Quote attributed to Louie Giglio.

Resources

Chapman, Gary. *The 5 Love Languages*. Chicago: Northfield Publishing, 1992.

Cook, Jerry, and Stanley Baldwin. *Love, Acceptance, and Forgiveness*. Glendale, CA: Regal Books, 1979.

Carter, Andre. *Fix My Man*. Montellus and Chloe Creations, 2016.

Goins, Brian. *Playing Hurt*. Grand Rapids: Kregel Publications, 2011.

Ferguson, Chuck, and Steve Duin. *Indomitable Spirit*. Portland, OR: Agora Publishing, 2004.

Foth, Dick, and Ruth Foth. *KNOWN*. New York: WaterBrook, 2017.

Goff, Bob. *Love Does*. Nashville: Thomas Nelson, 2012.

Jantz, Gregory L. *Battles Men Face*. Grand Rapids: Fleming H. Revell, 2012.

——— *Healing the Scars of Emotional Abuse*. Grand Rapids: Fleming H. Revell, 1995.

Hunter, James C. *The Servant*. New York: Crown Business, 1998.

Kirk, Jerry, with Stephen D. Eyre. *The Prayer Covenant*. Cincinnati: 40 Day Prayer Covenant Inc., 2013. Kindle.

Larson, Bruce. *No Longer Strangers*. Waco: Word Books, 1971.

Olsen, Terry. *My Father, My Hero*. Enumclaw, WA: Winepress Publishing, 1995.

Shedd, Charlie W. *Letters to Philip*. Old Tappan, NJ: Fleming H. Revell Co., 1973.

——— *Letters to Karen*. Nashville: Abingdon Press, 2012.

Smalley, Gary . *If Only He Knew*. Grand Rapids: Zondervan Publishing House, 2012.

Smalley, Gary, and John Trent. *The Language of Love*. Waco: Word Books, 1988.

Pumpkin Bundt Cake

- 3 cups sugar
- 2/3 cup shortening
- 1 ¾ cups pumpkin
- 4 eggs
- 2/3 cup water

I usually mix these 5 items in our Cuisinart mixer.

Mix in another bowl:
- 3 ½ cups flour
- 1 ½ tsp salt
- 2 tsp baking soda
- ½ tsp baking powder
- 1 tsp ground cinnamon
- ½ tsp ground cloves

Put this mixture in Cuisinart with the other mixture and mix up the batter.
Pour batter into greased Bundt pan. I usually grease it with Crisco before I start batter preparation.
Cook at 325 degrees for 45–60 minutes.
Makes 1 Bundt cake, 2 regular loaves, or 5 mini-loaves.

Order Information

REDEMPTION PRESS

*To order additional copies of this book, please visit
www.redemption-press.com.
Also available on Amazon.com and BarnesandNoble.com
Or by calling toll-free (844) 2REDEEM (273-3336).*

CPSIA information can be obtained
at www.ICGtesting.com
Printed in the USA
LVHW021708050120
642567LV00001B/142

9 781683 147701